# CANTERBURY STUDIES
# IN ANGLICANISM

## A Point of Balance

## The Weight and Measure of Anglicanism

# Also available in the same series

Apostolic Women, Apostolic Authority:
Transfiguring Leadership in Today's Church
*Martyn Percy & Christina Rees, Editors*

Calling on the Spirit in Unsettling Times:
Anglican Present and Future
*L. William Countryman*

Christ and Culture: Communion After Lambeth
*Martyn Percy, Mark Chapman, Ian S. Markham*
*& James Barney Hawkins IV, Editors*

Worship-Shaped Life Liturgical Formation and the People of God
*Ruth Meyers & Paul Gibson, Editors*

CANTERBURY STUDIES
IN ANGLICANISM

Series Editors: Martyn Percy and Ian Markham

# A Point of Balance

*The Weight and Measure of Anglicanism*

Edited by Robert Boak Slocum
and Martyn Percy

Morehouse Publishing
NEW YORK · HARRISBURG · DENVER

CANTERBURY
PRESS
Norwich

Morehouse Publishing
4775 Linglestown Road, Harrisburg, PA 17112

Morehouse Publishing
445 Fifth Avenue, New York, NY 10016

Morehouse Publishing is an imprint
of Church Publishing Incorporated.
www.churchpublishing.org

Cover design by Laurie Klein Westhafer
Typeset by Denise Hoff

Library of Congress Cataloging-in-Publication Data

A point of balance: the weight and measure of Anglicanism /
Robert Boak Slocum and Martyn Percy, editors.
    p. cm.
Includes bibliographical references.
ISBN 978-0-8192-2844-4 (pbk.) -- ISBN 978-0-8192-2845-1 (ebook)
1. Anglican Communion. I. Slocum, Robert Boak, 1952– II. Percy, Martyn.

BX5005.P65 2012
283.09'051--dc23

2012019994

Printed in the United States of America

10  9  8  7  6  5  4  3  2  1

*Ross*
*Same good for the*
*journey. God Bless*
*you in your walk.*

THIS VOLUME IS DEDICATED TO
those who live and those who study
the traditions of Anglicanism—
past, present, and yet to come.

# CONTENTS

# FOREWORD TO THE SERIES

*by Rowan Williams, Archbishop of Canterbury*

The question 'What is the real identity of Anglicanism?' has become more pressing and more complex than ever before in the last decade or so, ecumenically as well as internally. Is the Anglican identity a matter of firm Reformed or Calvinist principle, resting its authoritative appeal on a conviction about the sovereignty and all-sufficiency of Scripture interpreted literally? Is it a form of non-papal Catholicism, strongly focused on sacramental and ministerial continuity, valuing the heritage not only of primitive Christianity but also of mediaeval and even post-Reformation Catholic practice and devotion? Is it an essentially indeterminate Christian culture, particularly well adapted to the diversity of national and local sympathies and habits? Is the whole idea of an 'ism' misplaced here?

Each of these models has its defenders across the Communion; and each has some pretty immediate consequences for the polity and politics of the global Anglican family. Some long for a much more elaborately confessional model than has generally been the case—the sort of model that those who defined the boundaries of the Church of England in the sixteenth century were very wary of. Some are happy with the idea of the Communion becoming a federation of local bodies with perhaps, in the long run, quite markedly diverging theologies and disciplines. The disagreements over the ordination of women and the Church's response to lesbian and gay people have raised basic issues around the liberty of local churches to decide what are thought by many to be secondary matters; the problem then being that not everyone agrees that they are secondary. The question of identity is inseparable from the question of unity: to recognize another community as essentially the same, whatever divergences there may be in language and practice, is necessary for any unity that is more than formal—for a unity that issues in vigorous evangelism and consistent 'diaconal' service to the world.

And this means in turn that questions about Anglican identity will inevitably become questions about the very nature of the Church—and thus the nature of revelation and incarnation and the character of God's activity. I believe it is generally a piece of deplorably overheated rhetoric to describe those holding different views around the kind of questions I have mentioned as being adherents of 'different religions'; but there is an uncomfortable sense in which this exaggeration reminds us that the line between primary and secondary issues is not self-evidently clear—or at least that what we say about apparently secondary matters may reveal something about our primary commitments.

The long and short of it is that we should be cautious of saying of this or that development or practice 'It isn't Anglican', as if that settled the matter. One of the first tasks we need to pursue in the current climate is simply to look at what Anglicans say and do. We need to watch Anglicans worshipping, constructing patterns for decision making and administration, arguing over a variety of moral issues (not only sexuality), engaging in spiritual direction and the practices of private prayer. Without this, we shan't be in a good position to assess whether it's the same religion; and we are very likely to be assuming that what we take for granted is the norm for a whole church or family of churches.

The books in this series are attempts to do some of this 'watching'— not approaching the question of identity in the abstract but trying to discern how Anglicans identify themselves in their actual life together, locally and globally. I'd like to think that they might challenge some of the more unhelpful clichés that can be thrown around in debate, the stereotypes used by both Global South and Global North about each other. If it is true that— as I have sometimes argued in other places—true interfaith dialogue only begins as you watch the other when their faces are turned to God, this must be true a fortiori in the Christian context. And I hope that some of these essays will allow a bit of that sort of watching. If they do, they will have helped us turn away from the lethal temptation to talk always about others when our backs are turned to them (and to God).

We all know that simply mapping the plurality of what Anglicans do is not going to answer the basic question, of course. But it is a necessary discipline for our spiritual health. It is in the light of this that we can begin to think through the broader theological issues. Let's say for the sake of argument that church communities in diverse contexts with diverse convictions about some of the major issues of the day do as a matter of bare fact manage to acknowledge each other as Anglican disciples of Jesus Christ to the extent that they are able to share some resources in theological training and diaconal service: the task then is to try and tease out what—as a matter of bare fact—makes them recognizable to each other. Not yet quite theology, but a move towards it, and above all a move away from mythologies and projections.

If I had to sum up some of my own convictions about Anglican identity, I should, I think, have to begin with the fact that, at the beginning of the English Reformation, there was a widespread agreement that Catholic unity was secured not by any external structures alone but by the faithful ministration of Word and Sacrament—'faithful' in the sense of unadulterated by mediaeval agendas about supernatural priestly power or by the freedom of a hierarchical Church to add new doctrinal refinements to the deposit of faith. Yet as this evolved a little further, the Reformers in Britain turned away from a second-generation Calvinism which would have alarmed Calvin himself and which argued for a wholly literal application of biblical law to the present times and the exclusion from church practice of anything not contained in the plain words of Scripture. Gradually the significance of a continuous ministry in the historic style came more into focus as a vehicle of mutual recognition, eventually becoming the straightforward appeal to apostolic episcopal succession often thought to be a central characteristic of the Anglican tradition.

The blend of concern for ordered ministry (and thus ordered worship), freedom from an uncritical affirmation of hierarchical ecclesiastical authority, with the appeal to Scripture at the heart of this, and the rooted belief that the forms of common worship were the most important clues about what was held to be recognizably orthodox teaching—this blend or fusion came to define the Anglican ethos in a growing diversity of cultural contexts. Catholic, yes, in the sense of seeing the Church today as responsible to its history and to the gifts of God in the past, even those gifts given to people who have to be seen as in some ways in error. Reformed, yes, in the sense that the principle remains of subjecting the state of the Church at any given moment to the judgement of Scripture—though not necessarily therefore imagining that Scripture alone offers the answer to every contemporary question. And running through the treatment of these issues, a further assumption that renewal in Christ does not abolish but fulfils the long-frustrated capacities of human beings: that we are set free to sense and to think the texture of God's Wisdom in the whole of creation and at the same time to see how it is itself brought to fulfilment in the cross of Jesus.

This is the kind of definition that a sympathetic reading of the first two Anglican centuries might suggest. It certainly has implications for where we find the centre for such a definition in our own day. But the point is that it is a historical argument, not one from first principles; or rather, the principles emerge as the history is traced. Once again, it is about careful watching—not as an excuse for failing to look for a real theological centre but as a discipline of discerning the gifts that have actually been given to us as Anglicans.

Not many, I suspect, would seriously want to argue that the Anglican identity can be talked about without reference to Catholic creeds and ministry, or to think that a 'family' of churches can be spoken of without spelling out at least the essential family resemblances in terms of what Christ has uniquely done and what Christ continues to do in his Body through Word and Sacrament. But to understand how this does and does not, can and cannot, work, we need the kind of exact and imaginative study that this series offers us. I hope that many readers will take the trouble to work with the grain of such investigations, so that our life in the Communion (and in communion itself in its fullest sense, the communion of the Holy Spirit) will be enriched as well as calmed, and challenged as well as reinforced.

—*Rowan Cantuar:*
from Lambeth Palace, Advent 2009

# ABOUT THE CONTRIBUTORS

**Mark D. Chapman** is Vice-Principal of Ripon College Cuddesdon, Oxford, Reader in Modern Theology at the University of Oxford, and Visiting Professor at Oxford Brookes University. His most recent books are *Doing God: Religion and Public Policy in Brown's Britain* (2008) and *Bishops, Saints and Politics: Anglican Studies* (2007). He has written widely on modern church history and theology.

**A. Katherine Grieb** has taught New Testament at Virginia Theological Seminary since 1994. She previously taught at Bangor Theological Seminary in Maine. She cofounded the Pauline Soteriology Group at the Society for Biblical Literature, and served on the Board of the *Journal of Biblical Studies*. She was President of the Mid-Atlantic Region SBL in 2006–07. She also has served as a member of the Theology Committee of the House of Bishops of the Episcopal Church, and was appointed to the Faith and Order Commission of the World Council of Churches. She was one of seven theologians asked to write *To Set Our Hope on Christ*, in response to the Windsor Report. She is the author of *The Story of Romans: A Narrative Defense of God's Righteousness* (Westminster John Knox, 2002) and *Conversations with Scripture: Hebrews* (Anglican Association of Biblical Scholars, 2007).

**Robert D. Hughes** is Norma and Olan Mills Professor of Divinity and Professor of Systematic Theology at the School of Theology, Sewanee: The University of the South. His recent book, *Beloved Dust: Tides of the Spirit in the Christian Life*, received the Des Places Libermann award in Pneumatology from Duquesne University in 2010 and was short listed for the Michael Ramsey Prize in 2011. He has taught at Sewanee for thirty-four years, and published mostly in *Sewanee Theological Review* and *Anglican Theological Review*.

**Tom Hughson** was ordained a priest in the Society of Jesus in 1971. He held a faculty position in the Department of Theology at Marquette University from 1979, with the exception of 1986–89 as Dean at the Pontifical Biblical Institute-Jerusalem, and recently retired emeritus after some years as Director of Graduate Studies. Recent publications include "Interpreting Vatican II: 'A New Pentecost,'" *Theological Studies* 69 (2008); "From a Systematics of History to Communications: Transition, Difference, Options," in *Meaning and History in Systematic Theology: Essays in Honor of Robert M. Doran, SJ*, ed. J. Dadosky (Marquette University Press, 2009); "Social Justice and the

Common Good: What Are They For?" in *Catholic Social Teaching in Global Perspective,* ed. D. McDonald (Orbis, 2010); "Social Justice in Lactantius's Divine Institutes? An Exploration," in *Reading Patristic Texts on Social Ethics,* ed. B. Matz and J. Verstraeten (Catholic University of America, 2011). Involved in initiating the Society for the Study of Anglicanism, Hughson participates in annual meetings. He is at work on a book-length manuscript tentatively titled, "Christ and Society: Why Chalcedon Matters for Social Justice." He serves as Associate Editor of *Theological Studies.*

**Ann Loades** is Professor Emerita of Divinity, Department of Theology and Religion, and Honorary Professorial Fellow of St Chad's College, both University of Durham, and Honorary Professor in the School of Divinity, University of St. Andrews. She was the first woman in Durham to be awarded a professorship personal to herself, and only the second person to receive a Commander of the Most Excellent Order of the British Empire (CBE) for 'services to theology'. She is the author of *Feminist Theology: Voices from the Past,* and *Searching for Lost Coins: Explorations in Christianity and Feminism;* and co-editor of *Christology: Key Readings in Christian Thought.* She has written widely over a range of topics in Christian doctrine, philosophical and feminist theology, and has travelled and lectured in both mainland Europe and North America.

**Gerard Mannion** is Professor of Theology and Religious Studies, and Director of the Frances G. Center for Catholic Thought and Culture at the University of San Diego. His academic career has taken in posts in Oxford, Leeds, Liverpool (UK), and Leuven (Belgium). He has held visiting research fellowships at Union Theological Seminary, New York, and the Fondazione Bruno Kessler, Trento (Italy), as well as visiting professorships at the Universities of Tübingen (Germany) and Chichester (UK). He has published widely in the fields of both ecclesiology and ethics, as well as aspects of philosophy. His recent books include *Ecclesiology and Postmodernity: Questions for the Church in Our Time* (2007), *The Routledge Companion to the Christian Church* (ed., with Lewis Mudge, 2008), *The Ratzinger Reader* (ed., with Lieven Boeve, 2010), *John Calvin's Ecclesiology: Ecumenical Perspectives* (ed., with Eddy Van der Borght, 2011), and *A Teaching Church That Learns* (2012). He serves as Chair of the Ecclesiological Investigations International Research Network and Editor of the Continuum Series Ecclesiological Investigations. An Irish citizen, he is passionate about social justice, rugby union, travel, and music.

**Paula Nesbitt** is a Visiting Scholar at the Graduate Theological Union, Berkeley, California, where she is conducting research for the Anglican Communion's Continuing Indaba project as well as working on a longitudinal analysis of religious leadership and multiculturalism in the communion. Having researched the clergy occupation for twenty-five years, her publications include *Feminization of the Clergy in America: Occupational and Organizational Perspectives* (Oxford University Press, 1997), an edited volume, *Religion and Social Policy* (AltaMira Press, 2001), and numerous journal articles and book chapters. For the past ten years she taught as a Visiting Associate Professor in Sociology at the University of California, Berkeley. She also directed the Carl M. Williams Institute for Ethics and Values and taught at the University of Denver.

**Martyn Percy** is Principal of Ripon College Cuddesdon and the Oxford Ministry Course. He is also Professor of Theological Education at King's College London, and Professorial Research Fellow at Heythrop College London. He is also an Honorary Canon of Salisbury Cathedral. Martyn has served as a Director and Council member of the Advertising Standards Authority, as a Commissioner of the Direct Marketing Authority, and as an Adjudicator for the Portman Group (the self-regulating body for the alcoholic drinks industry). He is a member of the BBC Standing Committee on Religion and Beliefs, as well as an advisor to the British Board of Film Classification. Since 2003 he has coordinated the Society for the Study of Anglicanism at the American Academy of Religion. He writes on Christianity and contemporary culture, modern ecclesiology, and practical theology. His recent books include *Engaging Contemporary Culture: Christianity and the Concrete Church* (2005), *Clergy: The Origin of Species* (2006), and *Shaping the Church: The Promise of Implicit Theology* (2010).

**Philip Sheldrake** is Senior Research Fellow, Cambridge Theological Federation and Honorary Professor of University of Wales Trinity Saint David. He has written extensively on the interface of Christian spirituality, history, and public theology. He is currently writing on the city in Christian thought and on spirituality in contemporary usage. His most recent books are *Heaven in Ordinary: George Herbert & His Writings* (2009) and *Explorations in Spirituality: History, Theology & Social Practice* (2010). He is also involved internationally in interreligious dialogue.

**Robert Boak Slocum** is a Distinguished Lecturer in the Department of Philosophy and Religious Studies at St. Catharine College in Kentucky. He serves as Dean of the School of Arts and Sciences. He has served as President of the Society of Anglican and Lutheran Theologians, and he currently serves as a co-convenor of the Society for the Study of Anglicanism. He served on the editorial board of the *Anglican Theological Review*. He is the author of *Light in a Burning Glass: A Systematic Presentation of Austin Farrer's Theology* (2007); *The Theology of William Porcher DuBose: Life, Movement, and Being* (2000); and Editor of *A Heart for the Future: Writings on the Christian Hope* (2004). He served as Ecumenical Officer of the Episcopal Diocese of Lexington.

**Simon J. Taylor** studied theology in Oxford. He spent time as a research fellow of the Lincoln Theological Institute in Sheffield before being ordained. He is currently the Priest-in-Charge of St. Mary Redcliffe in Bristol. He cohosts a website, virtualtheology.net, which seeks to make theology accessible to a wide audience.

# ACKNOWLEDGEMENTS

The editors thank Victoria Slocum and Dr. Jenny Gaffin for technical assistance for the publication of this book, along with Natalie Watson of SCM-Canterbury Press. Their help and encouragement have been invaluable. We also thank all the presenters, panelists, contributors, and participants in the meetings and projects of the Society for the Study of Anglicanism during the past ten years.

# PREFACE

*Ann Loades*

The Society for the Study of Anglicanism was founded in 2003 by Martyn Percy and Tom Hughson (followed later by Rob Slocum), and the Society's remit is wide indeed, as these chapters show. It is evident that in quite unforeseen ways as Anglicanism became the name for a worldwide company of believers, Anglicanism would in many ways itself become an ecumenical experiment. A nineteenth-century coinage, it encompasses those in communion with the archbishop of Canterbury, who at the present time has to negotiate differences and difficulties within the Anglican Communion of an unprecedented kind. In this present volume, readers may be surprised to find essays by Roman Catholics, but the point of course is that we share spirituality, pastoral experience, spirituality in its reintegration with theology, across ecclesiastical boundaries. Moreover, it is as vital to have perspectives on a tradition from "without" as well as from "within"—and Roman Catholics apart, just who counts as one or the other may be a perplexing and contentious matter, as we all know. It is by no means easy to find the generosity to wish one another well when one has to face up to the likelihood that some issues cannot always be resolved, and the best one can hope for is to practice very demanding forms of patience, attentiveness, the scrupulous politeness of the very best diplomacy—and so much more, as the essayists in this collection so splendidly themselves exemplify, from very different locations. Exclusion of those with whom we most profoundly disagree as we live out of cultural and historical legacies we can as yet hardly comprehend are unlikely to serve the Anglican Communion well. And given the spread of understanding of religious traditions and learning amongst the laity in quite different ways across Christian communities worldwide, the hospitality of sympathy and trust shown to one another is likely to serve us better in the long run. There is much to learn.

# INTRODUCTION

## A Practical and Balanced Faith

*Robert Boak Slocum*

The past ten years brought many stresses and challenges to question the resilience of Anglican Communion, and those stresses are plainly visible in the chapters of this volume. Our contributors raise questions of authority and leadership (including the frequently repeated questions about who can be ordained, and who decides), questions of discipline and morality, questions of mission and relevance in a changing cultural landscape, questions of what it means to live Christian faith as an Anglican today. Throughout the Communion, and in these papers, there are varieties of perspectives to encounter.

Some inside and outside the Communion have despaired for the future, and wondered if the center would hold. Amos' question (3:3, KJV), "can two walk together, except they be agreed?" is relevant for the study of Anglicanism. The tradition has often shown how those who do not agree may yet find ways to walk together. But the question is as urgent and pressing today as it was in the time of Elizabeth and the Settlement, and there are plenty of issues to test and question us, many of them discussed in the chapters that follow this introduction.

Balance is at the heart of Anglican life and practice. It came with the Benedictine missionaries to England who brought a disciplined and practical life of prayer, labor, and study. They are our ancestors in Anglicanism, and we continue to live out of our Benedictine heritage. Centuries later we find in the *Laws of Ecclesiastical Polity* of Richard Hooker a balance of Scripture, tradition, and reason as sources of authority in Anglicanism. This allows interpretation of each of the three to be informed and corrected dynamically by the other two, so that no one of the three is understood in isolation from the others. Hooker himself was clear in upholding Anglican theology as distinct from Calvinism on the one hand and Roman Catholicism on the other, thereby balancing Anglicanism between different trajectories that he found less helpful.

As Anglicans we tend to be more pragmatic and occasional than systematic or speculative. The Elizabethan Settlement allows flexibility and local adaptation instead of dogmatism, and this approach continues to inform Anglicanism today. For example, the importance of local adaptation of theological principles is seen in the Chicago-Lambeth Quadrilateral, which provides that administration of the historic episcopate is to be locally adapted to the varying needs of nations and peoples called by God into the church. The tradition is practical and flexible in application. This pragmatism goes to the very core of Anglican identity. The Rule of St. Benedict states that all guests are to be received as Christ, and directs that the monastery utensils be treated like the sacred vessels of the altar. We may find the extraordinary in the ordinary and practical details of life.

Anglican theology can be likened to the English common law tradition in the sense that it favors a case-by-case application of a large body of understanding. It does not attempt an elaborate and systematic code of propositions to resolve questions before the fact. Instead of enormous *Summas*, some of the most significant writings in Anglican theology have been occasional in nature. For example, Charles Gore's *Lux Mundi* is a collection of essays on different topics—the Incarnation, the atonement, the Holy Spirit, the church—by various authors.

Some of the best samples of Anglican theology are found in sermon collections (such as those by Lancelot Andrewes, Phillips Brooks, and Austin Farrer), which represent the preacher's best efforts to apply theological reflection to the daily life of faith, whether in the context of celebrating Christmas Day, or a wedding, or the Nineteenth Sunday after Pentecost. The meaning of Christian faith is expressed in light of particular circumstances and needs, allowing a kind of "case method" that is individualized and adaptable. This method can be understood in terms of the virtue of prudence, and it is notably at odds with an *a priori* approach to religious understanding. The emphasis on the practical in Anglicanism is also seen in the fact that many of the most significant Anglican theologians and spiritual writers have been working pastors in parishes and not professional academics. For example, Hooker, George Herbert, and John Donne. They lived their field of study in a parish, and helped others do the same.

Anglicans are in Communion with the See of Canterbury, and pray together using the forms of the Prayer Book. If anyone asks what Anglicans believe about the meaning of human life and faith, or the Eucharist, or marriage, or death, the Prayer Book is the first and most definitive place to look. Theology is "done" in accordance with the texts of common prayer. The law of prayer is the law of belief. The Prayer Book allows considerable latitude for diversity within the essentials of Anglican theological understanding, and that diversity may be evident within an Anglican province, diocese, or parish.

Anglicanism is not a confessional faith that requires members to subscribe to a list of propositions or dogmas. Anglicanism is not an experiential faith that expects its members to have spoken in tongues or been slain in the spirit (although some may have had these experiences). But the experience of worship together—common prayer—is at the heart of Christian faith as practiced by Anglicans.

Anglican theology upholds the truth that God works through people, and in their daily lives. Jesus lived in the flesh, and it is through our own experience of living in the flesh, living in the world, that we find and are found by God. Hooker states that we participate in the life of Christ by receiving the sacraments, by sharing in the life of the church, by living the Christian life.

An emphasis on the Incarnation means that Anglicans can celebrate the beauty and wonder of creation, and the goodness of our own lives—our selves, our souls, and bodies. Our capacities of mind, body, and spirit are good gifts from God who loves us, even if our free will allows the possibility of misuse. Anglicans acknowledge the reality of sin. Most Anglicans participate in a General Confession of Sin at each Eucharist, and a form for Reconciliation of a Penitent is included in the Prayer Book as a sacramental rite. But Anglicanism is not sin-centered in outlook, or haunted by the specter of human depravity. Anglicans tend to be unafraid to think and choose for ourselves, using the gifts we have been given. For example, Anglicans tend to make their own decisions whether to drink alcohol or practice birth control.

As we live in the world and encounter the situations of daily life, we may be transformed in an ongoing way. Anglicans are more likely to say we are being saved than that we have been saved. This process may be likened to *theosis* in Orthodoxy, as we welcome God's life into our lives for transformation. As we dig deeper, we may discover more and more of the patristic roots of Anglicanism. This understanding was encouraged by the publication of the Library of the Fathers, through the efforts of Edward Pusey and others, which translated patristic texts into English. Michael Ramsey, 100th archbishop of Canterbury, likewise states that in times of conflict Christians are well advised to dig for the foundations, to keep going deeper until common ground is discovered.

Anglicanism makes no claim for infallibility at any time in theological pronouncements or biblical interpretations. The original version of the Articles of Religion affirmed that General Councils of the church may err, and have erred, even in things concerning God. The Anglican approach to apparent error has tended to allow time for sorting out disagreement instead of attempting to silence or squelch it. At times, no answer has been the best answer. This silence or inaction has been understandably maddening for some who wanted disputed questions to be settled immediately, and those ready to insist that the Communion "take a stand."

Anglicanism can be messy. It has loose ends, and unresolved questions. It calls for further discussion, and venues for ongoing discussion (including, I believe, the Society for the Study of Anglicanism). Sooner or later, we may discover that what draws us together is ever so much more powerful than what tears us apart. Sooner or later, we seek to find (and find again) a point of balance.

# 1

# THE BONDS AND LIMITS OF COMMUNION

## Fidelity, Diversity, and Conscience in Contemporary Anglicanism[1]

*Robert Boak Slocum*

Let me begin with a clarification about my method here. I'm taking some recent controversies in the Episcopal Church and the Anglican world as a kind of extended case study on the issue of conscience relative to the bonds and limits of shared communion in Anglicanism. I'm not here to argue the merits of recent controversies but to use these cases as occasions to reflect on ecclesiology in Anglicanism—how are we faithful to our calling to be the church together, how do we honor the truth and engage the life of community we have received, how do we make room and guard space for a variety of perspectives in the life of the church (or do we)?

In a sense, this topic and discussion evolved out of a clergy day I attended in 2010 in which Bishop Ted Gulick, former bishop of Kentucky (the "other diocese" in my state) and provisional bishop for the Episcopal Diocese of Fort Worth (the one in communion with the Episcopal Church), stated that the House of Bishops' 1977 Statement on Conscience at Port St. Lucie, Florida (drafted by the bishops' theology committee), was in effect a "grandfather clause" with applicability that didn't reach beyond the sitting bishops serving when it was passed, and didn't include those bishops who were subsequently consecrated, who at their ordinations promised to uphold the "doctrine, discipline, and worship" of an Episcopal Church that had committed itself to allow the ordination of women. Although I personally support and deeply appreciate Bishop Gulick's work in the Diocese of Fort Worth, and the difficulties he faced in working with a diocese whose bishop and diocesan convention sought to realign itself with another Anglican province more to its

---

1   This chapter is based on a presentation for the 2010 meeting of the Society for the Study of Anglicanism.

liking (the Anglican Province of the Southern Cone), I must admit to concern about his statement relative to the bishops' statement on conscience, and the role of conscience in the Episcopal Church.

The House of Bishops' Port St. Lucie statement on conscience was never enacted into canon by General Convention. But its provisions are significant for this discussion. A plain reading of the text does not suggest that its applicability was intended to be limited to bishops then serving. It acknowledges that we live "at a time when Episcopalians disagree on matters of great importance." It offers a basic summary of ecclesiology in Anglicanism, stating "the basic Anglican position has been to insist upon that which is clearly discerned from Scripture interpreted by the Tradition of the undivided Church, and enlightened by Spirit-guided reason, while refraining from the imposition of that which cannot be so demonstrated." The statement concludes that "one is not a disloyal Anglican if he or she abstains from implementing the decision [on the ordination of women to the priesthood] or continues to be convinced it was in error," and likewise acknowledges the problems of conscience that might be encountered by supporters of the ordination of women "when they find themselves in the minority in a diocese or parish."

The statement on conscience provides observations that urge respect for the conscience of others, "neither despising nor condemning those whose convictions differ from our own"; avoiding any pressure that "might lead a fellow Christian to contravene his or her conscience"; seeking an informed conscience for ourselves and others; patience; and trust that "our fellow Christians are indeed seeking the truth, even if we feel they could find it faster by just asking us." The observations section of the statement on conscience also makes an ecclesiological point in support of "the Anglican tradition which seeks to distinguish between what is required or not required of believers." It adds that "Anglican comprehensiveness is not just trying to be gentlemen (sic), not weak so-called 'tolerance,' and certainly not numbers-seeking."

This Anglican comprehensiveness means a willingness to distinguish what must be believed by a Christian from what "cannot be clearly demonstrated from basic Christian sources," along with an awareness and openness that "the Spirit leads the Church into further penetration of the Truth," and appreciation for the needed humility to admit we don't yet know what the church will be like when it reflects the full stature of Christ (Eph. 4:13).

The statement on conscience identifies the grave harm that results when the tension of comprehensiveness (perhaps even a union of opposites) is lost: "Leaving this Communion or forcing others to leave interferes with the process of searching together for that fuller penetration, for the truth."[2] Again, I see nothing in these observations and conclusions to indicate that the statement on conscience was a mere "grandfather clause." On the contrary, the statement points beyond the controversies of its time to a comprehensiveness and liberal inclusiveness that characterizes ecclesiology in Anglicanism at its best.

At about the time of Bishop Gulick's clergy day presentation, I also came across a short article by Ed Little, bishop of Northern Indiana, "Conscience Without Sunset," posted on September 25, 2009, by the Living Church News Service. Little (himself a self-described "strong supporter" of the ordination of women, who estimates that he has ordained more women than men during his episcopate) describes the Port St. Lucie statement as "a classic restatement of the priority of conscience when Christians disagree on matters of deep conviction," but he adds that it was "not to last."

The 1997 General Convention effectively declared objection to the ordination of women to be canonically illegal, making it impossible "to be ordained in the Episcopal Church if one cannot support women in all orders of ministry." Little notes that at the 1997 General Convention, many speeches in support of the change were concluded with the claim, "This is not a conscience issue. It's a justice issue." Little states that he grieves that "there is no longer a place in the church for those who cannot conscientiously support this practice." He wanted protections for conscience that were "without sunset," and not limited to grandfathers.

Little's concern is that the same pattern he witnessed with the Port St. Lucie statement and the ordination of women will again be seen relative to the opponents of ordination of homosexuals, and same sex blessings. Little states, "Not immediately . . . but someday people like me will find ourselves on the margins, without the ability to test a vocation to ordained ministry, our position banned, theological uniformity imposed." He quotes a question by Lord Carey of Clifton, the 103rd archbishop of Canterbury, "Can conservative believers be assured that they have a future place in TEC without censure or opposition?" It's a fair question that calls for a liberal response. And if the best answer proves to be that conservatives may find a place in the Episcopal Church that's not without opposition, but is without censure, perhaps one out of two isn't bad.

William Porcher DuBose, an Episcopal theologian of the late nineteenth and early twentieth centuries, wrote an essay titled "Evangelical and Catholic, Each Needs the Other, Both Need the Church, and the Church Needs Both." It was published posthumously in 1920 in *The Constructive Quarterly*, an ecumenical journal, and it makes explicit his liberal and inclusive vision for the

---

2   See "Statement of Conscience, 1977," in Donald S. Armentrout and Robert Boak Slocum, eds., *Documents of Witness, A History of the Episcopal Church, 1782–1985* (New York: Church Hymnal Corporation, 1994), 599–602; Journal of General Convention, 1979, B193–B195. The statement was adopted at a Special Meeting of the House of Bishops, Port St. Lucie, Florida, October 3, 1977.

church. He urges that "for Christianity as a whole, there has to be, not alone a consent 'to live and let live,' but a deeper understanding, a truer union, and a more real sense of oneness between Evangelical and Catholic." This is much more than a benign toleration of opposing tendencies because "each side needs all the true emphasis of the other for more than correction—for completion of itself."[3]

In another *Constructive Quarterly* essay, "A Constructive Treatment of Christianity," DuBose sharply criticized the evil of sects in Christianity as "organized and isolated differences and diversities," and he lamented the loss to the church as a whole due to sectarianism: "Their partial and emphasized good is withdrawn from communication to and influence upon others; their deficiencies, ignorances or errors are removed from supplementing or correction by others." Separation, isolation, or schism of members of the church from one another is therefore a great loss to the church, and all the members who are deprived of each other. In his *Constructive Quarterly* essay "The Church," DuBose states that the church is "divinely organized and constituted Unity" in which "by free interrelation and interaction different points of view, impressions, emphases, perspectives, and so theories, doctrines, systems, etc. may correct, supplement, and complete one another and bring all to the essential and sufficient unity that not only belongs to them but can come only through their all-sided contributions."[4] This makes for a very liberal and inclusive perspective on the church: each needs the other, all sides need each other, and the church needs them all.

We cannot afford to say to another in the church, "I have no need of you" (1 Cor. 12:22), even another with whom we may disagree strongly. It seems clear that DuBose would heartily agree with the statement on conscience that "leaving this Communion or forcing others to leave interferes with the process of searching together for truth." Our collective discerning may be helped by a diversity of perspectives and ways of seeing. We need each other, and the church needs us, even when we disagree, and even when continuing relationship is very challenging. Schism diminishes us all.

Bishop Little mentioned in a 2010 conversation that the Episcopal Church's House of Bishops' was considering ways to provide "safe spaces" for theological minorities. He hoped for a response that would be canonical and structural in the church as well as pastoral, so that those in a minority position could remain in the church and be assured that their positions would be honored. He noted that a small group of bishops representing the full spectrum

---

3  William Porcher DuBose, "Evangelical and Catholic, Each Needs the Other: Both Need the Church and the Church Needs Both," in W. Norman Pittenger, ed., *Unity in the Faith* (Greenwich, CT: Seabury Press, 1957): 188–205, 205. This essay was originally published in 1920 in the *Constructive Quarterly: A Journal of the Faith, Work, and Thought of Christendom*, an ecumenical quarterly. See *Constructive Quarterly* 8, no. 3 (September 1920): 345–362. See also Robert Boak Slocum, *The Theology of William Porcher DuBose: Life, Movement and Being* (Columbia, SC: University of South Carolina Press, 2000), especially 4–5, 14, 102–106.

4  William Porcher DuBose, "A Constructive Treatment of Christianity," in Pittenger, ed., *Unity in the Faith*: 35–51, 36–37.

of the church "from right to left" were meeting to explore various models and approaches to protect conscience. Bishop Little also hoped for "ministerial reproduction," so that ordination of those holding minority positions would be possible. In this context, he noted that those opposed to the ordination of women have themselves been technically barred from ordination in the Episcopal Church since 1997. Bishop Little likewise emphasized that any conscience provision "must cut both ways," serving to protect conservatives in a predominantly liberal jurisdiction, and to protect liberals in a predominantly conservative jurisdiction.

Bishop Little voiced one additional concern that deserves to be shared. He observed that the Episcopal Church seems to be following secular politics in terms of how to deal with opponents, where the tendency is to defeat and discredit opponents and remove them from office, instead of "keeping the tent as broad as possible." This tendency is easy to observe in American culture, especially during a presidential campaign that is marked by negativity and personal attacks.

Little raises important ecclesiological questions concerning the place of disagreement and dissent (and dissenters) in the life of the church, and the futility of trying to nail down just exactly what Anglicans must and must not believe in matters not addressed by the historic creeds. Austin Farrer once preached in his sermon "Double Thinking" that it would be well for the church to listen even to "our own heretics" and seek to understand what drove them into heresy, instead of being most concerned to condemn and suppress them.[5] I offer this statement, of course, not to associate Bishop Little or those who share his perspectives or anyone I've mentioned today with heresy (I don't!), but to remind that the church as a whole can learn from and be enriched by all kinds of sources, and that schism is a greater threat to the church than even heresy. As we state in the Prayer Book Catechism, "The mission of the Church is to restore all people to unity with God and each other in Christ."[6] All people. This mission is severely impaired if we break away from each other, and end our conversations.

In DuBose's essay "Liberty and Authority in Christian Truth," he warns against "the impossibility of extinguishing error by legislation or banishing it by exclusion, or getting rid of it in any other way than by meeting and overcoming it with the truth." Indeed, DuBose states, the "best expulsion of error is through the freedom permitted to it of self-exposure," and "the ultimate best, if not only, method of eliminating error" is by causing it "to meet and be overcome by truth."[7] In this regard, we may recall that Anglicanism (as we have known it) is at least so far without a binding confession of faith or a

---

5   Austin Farrer, "Double Thinking," in Austin Farrer, *A Celebration of Faith* (London: Hodder and Stoughton, 1970): 26–30, 26. See Robert Boak Slocum, *Light in a Burning-Glass: A Systematic Presentation of Austin Farrer's Theology* (Columbia, SC: University of South Carolina Press, 2007), especially 24–28.

6   *The Book of Common Prayer* (New York: Church Hymnal Corporation, 1979), 855.

7   William Porcher DuBose, "Liberty and Authority in Christian Truth," in William Porcher DuBose, *Turning Points in My Life* (New York: Longmans, Green & Co., 1912): 125–143, 140.

magisterium to ban or silence individual dissent, but we may need to be on guard against subtler ways that achieve the same result.

For instance, in 2010 there was a lively conversation online about controversial issues, statements, and positions potentially relevant for the canonical consent process of a conservative bishop-elect in the Episcopal Church, Dan Martins, who was elected bishop of Springfield. In this context, Jennifer Phillips, from Rhode Island, reflected online concerning the historic church's history of controversy, in which sometimes the theologies of heretics have proven useful to the mainstream and preserved "some strand of thought about God or some part of the ancient conversation that has value." She added this advice to the discussion: "Here, I believe, we might do well to embrace some of the tradition of our Jewish neighbors and preserve the rabbinic debate around the margins of the sacred texts, understanding that the truth does not reside in one opinion or the other, but in the conversation of learned and reverent voices over time as they seek to discern the energy and will of the Holy One in the midst of them." And in the meantime, I would add, we must *listen* to each other, and make room for each other. As DuBose states in *The Gospel According to St. Paul*, "We shall gratefully acknowledge one another's contributions of truth, whatever they may be; and we shall not content ourselves with anathematizing one another's shortcomings or errors."[8] I hope not.

In a context of controversy, one may uphold one's own truth in a way that does not take into account the truths of an opposing perspective, and that overlooks the partial truths and potential weaknesses of one's own perspective. For example, DuBose notes in his book *The Ecumenical Councils* concerning the controversy over Nestorianism at the Council of Ephesus (431) that "Cyril is singularly clear and sound in detecting the logical tendencies and dangers of the opposite side, but of the possibility of a contribution of truth from that direction such as was to be recognized and accepted in the Council of Chalcedon, he and his party seem as yet to have caught no inkling."[9]

Even if the truth of a particular perspective is incomplete, it may still be valuable to the extent that it is true, and the church would be deprived by the effective loss of that perspective. The paradoxes and inconsistencies of spiritual truth can only be comprehended in the context of sharing different perspectives within the community, and this must be done with a view to the larger comprehension and discernment of the church, which includes and surpasses individual perspectives. As DuBose states, "Only such a complex resultant of the operation of many minds and lives as we have in the Scriptures or in the church can combine the whole truth or express the sum of Christian experience." DuBose also states in *The Ecumenical Councils*

---

8   William Porcher DuBose, *The Gospel According to St. Paul* (New York: Longmans, Green & Co., 1907), 13.

9   William Porcher DuBose, The Ecumenical Councils, vol. 3 of *Ten Epochs of Church History*, ed. John Fulton (New York: Christian Literature Company, 1896), 233–234.

that "the collective mind" of the church will "sooner or later" exclude what is spiritually false and include what is spiritually true.[10] This must be done by the church as a whole over an extended period of shared life and reflection. Reception takes time. In the meantime, we listen to each other, and make room for each other.

Each needs the other—as we engage different and perhaps sharply opposing perspectives, as we hope to discern together in a comprehensive way over time—and the church needs *all*.

---

10  *Ibid.*, 28, 321.

# 2

# ENGAGEMENT, DIVERSITY, AND DISTINCTIVENESS

## Anglicanism in Contemporary Culture

*Martyn Percy*

Let me, if I may, try and capture something of the issues we might face as a church and as a Communion in a single vignette that might begin to illustrate something of the nature of cultural shifts with which we are engaging. As I drove purposefully down the road on a wet April evening in 2003, I was already slightly late (as usual) for picking up my son from Cubs. But there was no need to panic, I mused, since the ever-enthusiastic Cub leader normally overran the meetings by at least ten to fifteen minutes. Sure enough, I arrived at the entrance to the church hall to discover a group of parents waiting somewhat tardily for their offspring to come out.

But as I joined the small throng to show solidarity in patience, I realised I had walked into a reasonably terse discussion. Each parent was clutching a letter from *Akela*, which reminded parents and Cubs that Sunday was St. George's Day, and that Cubs were expected (indeed, the letter stated that it was "compulsory") to attend church parade. Smart kit and clean shoes were also recommended. The parents stood around, discussing the word "compulsory." One looked bewildered, and cast around for empathy as he explained that his son played soccer on Sunday, so attendance was doubtful. Another mused that the family were all due to be away for the weekend, and that changing plans for a church parade was neither possible nor desirable. Another looked less than pleased that a "voluntary" organisation such as the Cubs, which she added her son went to by choice, should now be using words like "compulsory." There was no question of obligation; attendance and belonging was a matter of preference.

At the beginning of the twenty-first century, a small vignette such as this would not be untypical in Western Europe. In the postwar era, a nascent culture of obligation has rapidly given way to one of consumerism. Duty, and the desire to participate in aspects of civic society where steadfast obligatory support was once cherished, has been rapidly eroded by choice, individualism, and reflexivity. Granted, this is not the place to debate such a cultural turn. But its undoubted appearance on the landscape of late modernity has posed some interesting questions for voluntary organisations, chief of which might be religious establishments. Increasingly, churches find themselves with worshippers who come less out of duty and more out of choice. There is, arguably, nothing wrong with that. But under these new cultural conditions, churches have discovered that they need to have much more savvy about how they shape and market themselves in the public sphere. There is no escaping the reality: the churches are in competition: for people's time, energy, attention, money, and commitment.

But it is that last word, "commitment," that has become such a slippery term in recent times. Few regular or frequent churchgoers now attend church twice on a Sunday, which was once normal practice. For most, once is enough. Many who do attend on a regular basis are now attending less frequently. Even allowing for holidays and other absences, even the most dedicated churchgoer may only be present in church for 70 percent of the Sundays in any given year. Many clergy now remark on the decline in attendance at Days of Obligation (i.e., major saints days, or feast days such as the Ascension). The Committed, it seems, are also the busy. The response to this from amongst the more liturgical churches has been to subtly and quietly adapt their practice, whilst preserving the core tradition. For example, the celebration of Epiphany may now take place on the Sunday nearest to January 6th, and not on the day itself. A number of Roman Catholic churches now offer Sunday Mass on Saturday evenings, in order for Sunday to be left as a family day, or for whatever other commitments or consumerist choices that might now fall on the once hallowed day of rest. The phrase "our duty and our joy" has been, arguably, replaced in our consciousness with "our choice, and at our pleasure—time permitting."

In such a context, religion undoubtedly lives—but no longer as a meta-narrative. It is, rather, one of the many ideologies and activities that compete for time and interest in an increasingly ephemeral public sphere. Under such conditions, churches and theology have at least three tasks. First, to be able to "higgle"—the old English (agricultural) word that describes the process of continuing to affect things by degrees. Second, to be able to "thole"—an old Irish word that describes the process of survival under adverse conditions (i.e., "tholing" through bad times at work, or perhaps through a difficult relationship). Third, to be engaged in renewal. Now, renewal can be read in two senses here. Renewal can mean a process of recovery and restoration, but it can also mean replacement. Here I want to suggest that both senses are implied for the churches and theology today. The Christian tradition must face the present and the future with courage, but it cannot neglect its past.

There is scope for exploring radical diversity, but this must be pursued with a heed to maintain continuity.

Put another way, we might say that Christianity has to pursue its engagement with the world through a combination of resistance and accommodation. In a quite fundamental and deep way, this is something that Jesus draws our attention to through his telling analogy, found in the gospels:

> You are the salt of the earth; but if the salt loses its strength, by what shall it be salted? It will be strong for nothing except to be cast away and trodden underfoot by men. (Matt. 5:13, author's translation)

In interpreting this text, a majority of bible commentators work with a false assumption, namely that the "salt" in this text is the white granular chemical we know as sodium chloride, where its purpose is to add flavour to foods, or occasionally to act as a purifier or preservative. But the "salt" that Jesus is referring to here is actually a saltlike material or mineral such as potash or phosphate. These *halas* elements were available in abundance in and around the Dead Sea area of Palestine, and were used for fertilising the land and enriching the manure pile, which was then spread on the land.

This way of understanding the *halas* of the metaphor changes the sense of the text significantly. The "salt" is not to be kept apart from society, and neither is it to be used as a purifier or as an additive stabiliser. The "salt" of Jesus' metaphor is a mutating but coherent agent that is both distinct yet diffusive in its self-expenditure. As a result of individuals, communities, values, witness, and presence—the *halas*—being literally dug into society, the earth or soil will benefit, and many forms of life can then flourish. There is a temporal dimension here: what must begin as distinct and powerful to be useful ends up being absorbed and lost. Of course, this reading of the metaphor makes sense of Jesus' own self-understanding, which in turn is reflected in his parables, teachings, and other activities. So if the church or the disciples of Jesus are the salt of the earth, they will begin by being a distinct yet essential component within society, but who will ultimately fulfill their vocation through engaging self-expenditure. The power of salt is that it is pervasive, and nourishing—it expends itself by giving life to others.

## About Being, Not Just Doing

I realize that the salt metaphor in relation to culture might sound a little too passive, but let me press this a little further with a different but related analogy. I have recently been enjoying a new book called *What Mothers Do*, by Naomi Stadlen. Intriguingly, the book is subtitled: "Especially When It Looks Like Nothing." *What Mothers Do: Especially When It Looks Like Nothing*? Her argument is beautifully simple. She says that contemporary culture is mesmerisingly gripped by formulae and recipes, which seldom correspond to the reality of the ingredients. So-called "Mother and Baby" books are a good

15

example: they offer step-by-step advice, which appears to be simple and effective. But, argues Stadlen, most of these kinds of books infantalise the mother. What happens if I have a baby that doesn't do what the book says? Guilt, frustration, and anger can quickly set in. Or try another book: but then, what happens if that also fails to mould the child in the image of the author? The "how-to" books, says Stadlen, reduce motherhood to a series of tasks, instead of concentrating on the relationship between mother and child. (Most mother and baby books are, by the way, written by men—about 75 percent of them.) She argues that mothers rarely need to be told how to care; it is learned and developed in and through relationships, not through advice-lines and programmatic books.

The heart of the book suggests that mothers are always doing something with their offspring, and most especially when it looks like nothing. They are *engaged* with their child. They are relating. They are being with and being for the child. So the question "what have you done today"—often asked of a young mother—needs no obvious reply, even though it often prompts guilt and embarrassment. To simply have been with the child is ample; to have discovered a song or a sound that comforts him; or something visual that simply amuses and stimulates her. This is enough.

It seems to me that one of the most pressing problems that beset the church today is that it too is gripped by a culture of formulae. Many ecclesial recipe books have appeared in recent times: *How to Grow your Church*; *How to Manage your Congregation*; *Mission Shaped Church*; *The Purpose-Driven Church*; or Alpha Courses; and who can forget "the decade of evangelism"? Each of these initiatives is well-meaning, but also deeply in the thrall of the formulaic; it can sometimes look like a kind of panacea for panickers. Clergy are easily seduced by such things. Many wince at Christmas when someone sidles up to them at a drinks party and says: "So, Vicar, your busy time then." Because the flip side of the question often asked of clergy is also implied by this remark: "What exactly do you do all day, Vicar?"

Clergy are often stumped for an answer. Communion in a residential home for five elderly people, a couple of visits, some paperwork, morning and evening prayer, one meeting, and perhaps a bit of time for thinking doesn't sound like a very productive day. But here clergy are at one with mothers. They have been doing a lot: it just seems like nothing. They have deepened and kindled relationships. They have related to many people for whom dependency is a fact of life, concentrating deeply on being, not just doing. They have made somebody's day, simply by dropping by, or by smiling.

In reflecting on this sense of achieving nothing, despite having expended a great deal of effort caring for the baby, Hannah Arendt's discussion of the difference between *labour* and *work* is particularly helpful. In her *Human Condition* (1958) she describes labour as being driven by the necessity to sustain life. It is, by definition, repetitive; and its effort is consumed because it is not about producing things, but is directed towards maintaining life. Work, on the other hand, is driven by ideas and aims towards making things that are tangible and durable; the effort is put into the making of an end.

The work of mothering is labour. It is a repetitive cycle of effort driven by the desire and necessity of sustaining the life of the child. Our present culture is deeply committed to valuing work over labour, even when the "products" of work are in fact made for our consumption. We speak (all too easily) of "working mothers," and in so doing send a message that while a mother is engaged in full-time childcare, she is not, *per se*, "working." We do not have the words to affirm the effort that goes into the being with and caring of, that is central to a baby's well-being. As Stadlen says: "When they look at a mother sitting quietly with her baby, they cannot see much going on. It's not most people's idea of doing a mother's work" (*What Mothers Do*, 83).

Similarly, and in the past when clergy had a certain status, there was rarely a need to justify what it was that a priest did beyond the provision of services. Yet in today's climate, clergy can often feel a desire to produce some tangible sign of the effort they are putting into ministry. This is particularly difficult for clergy who see a significant part of ministry being about building relationships, and being available to the needy. How do you quantify the value of visiting the housebound, or sitting in the toddler group and talking to new mums? How do you quantify time spent with the bereaved or the dying? Anecdotally, time spent is affirmed by assurance that one's presence has been of inestimable help; but rarely is there anything tangible to show. Good pastorally orientated clergy tend to be very busy, but the busyness doesn't always look like "work."

So formulas, like recipes, anticipate success, and churches are usually too tempted to worship both the rubric and the outcome. But unlike recipe books, courses and books that address the apparent malaise of the church forget that just as every child is different, so is every congregation: a uniquely constituted set of ingredients. What works in one place probably won't in another. So the moral of this analogy is simple. Don't impose formulae or strategies for growth on children or churches, and don't try and cook up congregations or dioceses in the same way that you might try and cook up some food. Respect what has come naturally, and work with that. Even if that simply means just being, and apparently doing nothing: there is something to be said for having confidence in being, not just doing.

It would, of course, take some confidence to concentrate on being rather than doing, and yes, I know they can't be easily divided: being is its own kind of doing, to be sure. But Stadlen's cultural theory suggests to me, at least, that there is merit in focusing less on what we do and more on what we are actually about. And support for this idea comes from two unlikely sources: one a theologian (Karl Barth) and the other a sociologist (David Martin). Taking Barth first, he writes:

> The true growth which is the secret of the up-building of the community is not extensive but intensive; its vertical growth in height and

depth. . . . It is not the case that its intensive increase necessarily involves an extensive. We cannot, therefore, strive for vertical renewal merely to produce greater horizontal extension and a wider audience. . . If it [the Church and its mission] is used only as a means of extensive renewal, the internal will at once lose its meaning and power. It can be fulfilled only for its own sake, and then—unplanned and unarranged—it will bear its own fruits.[1]

Here Barth is saying something very simple: true growth can only come through the quality of our relationship with God. And sometimes, in terms of extensive growth, that will appear to be fruitless. But this is precisely the point where we are called to contemplative persistence rather than pragmatism, and to question ourselves before we embark on a headlong rush into a search for new formulae or another strategy for our churches or diocese. Barth steers us away from this, quite rightly in my view, by reminding us that first and foremost we are to be for God, before we are busy for clarity, success, and ambition for the kingdom.

In a similar vein, David Martin reminds us that the division between maintenance and mission is essentially a false one. As any dean knows, a beautifully kept cathedral (or greater parish church) is, de facto, a sign of mission and a pointer to the kingdom. Active maintenance through gradual renewal is a form of mission, just as letting church buildings decline, collapse, or simply appear shabby in the public sphere constitutes a very poor advert, suggesting that the church cannot take care of itself. Churches, in other words, can represent our being before God. Martin writes:

Not only are they [i.e., churches] markers and anchors, but also the only repositories of all-embracing meanings pointing beyond the immediate to the ultimate. They are the only institutions that deal in tears and concern themselves with the breaking points of human existence. They provide frames of reference and narratives and signs to live by and offer persistent points of reference.[2]

This, of course, raises some fascinating questions for us as a church. How are we to continue being "a persistent point of reference"? How do we adapt and survive as a church or Communion? How are we to manage ourselves, and can we really afford to concentrate more on being and less on doing? Can we really risk a focus that looks more on our identity and less on our activity? How are we to engage with difference and disagreement? I don't have all the answers to these questions, as you'd expect, but here are three modest proposals in the first instance.

First, it is probably the case that Anglicanism is easier to identify through

---

1   Karl Barth, *The Church Dogmatics*, Book IV, volume 2 (Edinburgh: T & T Clark, 1958), chapter 15, p. 648.

2   David Martin, from an unpublished paper, and quoted in Grace Davie, *Religion in Britain Since 1945: Believing Without Belonging* (Oxford: Blackwell, 1994).

persons rather than systems: *examples* of faith and polity rather than theories of it. In view of this, I'd be inclined to say that the practice of our faith is more of an art than a science, and most especially in relation to problem-solving. Here, the "management" of the church within the context of the challenges of contemporary culture is much more like a "knack" than a skill; organizing or shaping the church is about learned habits of wisdom more than it is about rules and theories.[3]

Second, those charged with the ministry of oversight—in both sacred and secular spheres—often speak of *intuition* rather than extended calculation or analysis when dealing with "unique situations to which they must respond under conditions of stress and limited time."[4] This "knack" or "wisdom" depends, as Polanyi might say, on "tacit knowing," where overseers seldom turn to theories or methods in managing situations, but instead realize that their own effectiveness depends on having learnt (and continuing to learn) through the "long and varied practice in the analysis of . . . problems, which builds up a generic, essentially un-analyzable capacity for problem-solving."[5] In other words, we learn by experience in the field.

Third, I'd suggest that the outcome of this has important implications for the collegiality of those engaged in the task of oversight. It is in *sharing*—quite deeply, I think, and at quite a personal level—how problems are addressed and resolved, and how individuals and organizations fare in this, and what reflections or analysis one may have, that "tacit knowledge" is built up—within relationships based on trust—such that the organization may then experience both stability and a degree of transcendence. What I think does not work is the devolving of more power and authority to semi-detached "systems" of governance or theories of leadership, no matter how worthy or novel. Granted, these may have their uses, but I would remind us that Anglicanism remains stubbornly identifiable through persons not systems. Correspondingly, it is how we "hold" issues, the character we exhibit under pressure, and how we continue to embody being the very best kinds of "reflective practitioner" that may help the church most as it seeks to address the multiple complexities of being within contemporary culture. Put simply: I'd suggest we need a little more collegiality and the communion of shared wisdom; and perhaps a little less emphasis on science and formulae.

## Anglican Distinctiveness and Cultural Diversity

With these comments in mind, let me say something about Anglican distinctiveness in the midst of cultural diversity. It would be quite possible here to talk at length about our explicit theological identity. But I prefer instead to address a few aspects of what I take to be our anthropological identity, which

---

3  C.f. Donald Schon, *The Reflective Practitioner* (London: Ashgate, 1991).
4  *Ibid.*, p. 239.
5  *Ibid.*

in turn suggests a nascent value-based implicit theological shape. It is said that Henry Scott Holland once stood on the hill at Garsington shortly before his death, and gazed over the valley to Cuddesdon College and parish church, where he had asked to be buried. He noticed a flock of starlings flying past, and remarked how like the Anglican Church they were. Nothing, it seemed, kept the flock together—and yet the birds moved as one, even though they were all apart and retained their individual identity. In an increasingly diverse and cosmopolitan world, of which the Anglican Communion is a part, birds of a feather still need to flock together, even though each creature is individual.

Holland's observation allows us to develop another analogy here, centered on the identity of the species. The Anglicanism of the twenty-first century is recognisably different from that of the end of the nineteenth century. The flock, if you like, is no longer one type of bird. Evolution—through cultural and theological diversity—has meant that many Anglican provinces have evolved to "fit" their contexts, and the ultimate diversity of the species clearly threatens its unity. But to extend the analogy just a little further, is it possible to still speak of a connecting DNA—some of the deep core, but hidden constituents of our identity which relate us, even though they may not be immediately apparent?

It was Jeremy Paxman who once quipped that the Church of England is the kind of body that believes that there was no issue that could not be eventually solved over a cup of tea in the vicar's study. This waspish compliment directed towards Anglican polity serves to remind us that many regard its ecclesial praxis as being quintessentially peaceable and polite, in which matters never really get too out of hand. For similar reasons, Robert Runcie once described Anglican polity as a matter of "passionate coolness." In the past, and in my own reflections on Anglican polity, these are sentiments with which I have tended to concur:

> In some of my conversations with Anglican theologians . . . I have been struck by how much of the coherence of Anglicanism depends on good manners. This sounds, at face value, like an extraordinarily elitist statement. It is clearly not meant to be that. What I mean by manners is learning to speak well, behave well, and be able to conduct yourself with integrity in the midst of an argument. . . . It is often the case that in Anglicans' disputes about doctrine, order or faith, it is actually the means that matter more than the ends. . . . Politeness, integrity, restraint, diplomacy, patience, a willingness to listen, and above all, not to be ill-mannered—these are the things that enable the Anglican Communion to cohere.[6]

In macrotheological disputes, such as those over the ordination of women, part of the strategy that enables unity can be centred on containing some of

---

6   Martyn Percy, *Shaping the Church: The Promise of Implicit Theology* (London: Ashgate, 2010), p. 144.

the more passionate voices in the debate. Extreme feelings, when voiced, can lead to extreme reactions. And extreme reactions, when allowed full vent, can make situations unstable. Nations fall apart; communions fracture; families divide. Things said briefly in the heat of a moment can cause wounds that may take years to heal. What is uttered is not easily retracted. Good manners, then, is not a bad analogy for "ideal" Anglican polity. In a church that sets out to accommodate many different peoples of every theological hue, there has to be a foundation—no matter how implicit—that enables the Communion to cohere across party lines, tribal borders, and doctrinal differences. And just as this is true for macrotheological disputes, so is it also true for microecclesial squabbles. Often congregational unity in the midst of disputes can only be secured by finding a middle open way, in which the voices of moderation and tolerance occupy the central ground and enable a church to move forwards. This is something that the *Windsor Report* understands, and it is interesting to note how much attention the Report gives to the virtues of patience and restraint, whilst also acknowledging the place of passions and emotions in the sexuality debate. Clearly, there is a tension between these polarities (the polite-passionate axis), which is partly why the cultivation of "mannered-ness" in ecclesial polity can be seen as being as essential as it is beguiling.

This means, of course, continually listening to the experiences that lead to anger, and seeing them as far as possible from the perspective of those with less power. It means humility on the part of those who hold power, and an acknowledgment of the fear of losing power and control. It means a new way of looking at power relationships that takes the gospel seriously in their equalising and levelling. I am aware that this is one of the most demanding aspects of oversight, namely having the emotional intelligence, patience, and empathy to hold feelings, anger, disappointment, and frustration—other people's, as well as your own. Episcopacy, it seems to me, is less about strategy and more about (deeply learnt) poise, especially in holding together competing convictions and trying to resolve deep conflicts.

But before conflicts can be resolved, they must first of all be *held*. And here we find another of the most demanding aspects of oversight within the context of considerable theological and cultural diversity. Because one of the tasks of the church is to soak up sharp and contested issues, in such a way as to limit and blunt the possibility of deep intra- and interpersonal damage being caused, as well as further dislocation in people's sense of faithful identity. Retaining composure, and somehow holding people together who would otherwise divide (due to the nature of their intense and competing convictions), is a stretching vocation. Anyone exercising a ministry of oversight will understand the costly nature of this vocation—a kind of servant leadership—that understands that much of Anglican polity is "open" in its texture, and although it has a shape, is nonetheless unresolved and incomplete. Therefore, issues that cannot be determined often require being held, a deliberate postponement of resolution. Put another way, there is a tension between being an identifiable community with creeds and fundaments, and yet also being a body that recognises that some issues are essentially undecidable in the church. Indeed, "Anglican undecidability" (a phrase coined by Stephen Pickard) may turn out to be one of the chief countercultural Anglican virtues; it is very far from being a problem, as some appear to believe.

The desire and need to sometimes reach settlements that do not achieve closure is itself part of the deep "habit of wisdom" that has helped to form Anglican polity down the centuries. It is embodied liturgically in the Book of Common Prayer, but can also be traced in pastoral, parish, and synodical resolutions that cover a significant range of issues. Essentially, this "calling" is about inhabiting the gap between vocation, ideals, praxis, and action. No neutral or universally affirmed final settlements can be reached on a considerable number of issues within the church. But provisional settlements have to be reached that allow for the possibility of continuing openness, adjustment, and innovation. Inevitably, therefore, any consensus is a slow and painful *moment* to arrive at, and even when achieved, will usually involve a degree of provisionality and more open-endedness. This is, of course, a typical Anglican habit, embodying a necessary humility and holiness in relation to matters of truth, but without losing sight of the fact that difficult *decisions* still need to be made.

In this respect, the Scriptures are of course helpful and vital in guiding the church through this complex dimension of its polity. Decisions often involve an irrevocable commitment to the future, which in turn can require obedience rather than dissent. This, of course, places a further and heightened value on undecidability, since this allows for the continuance of courtesy and hospitality, which is essential in a Communion that embodies so much diversity. Paula Nesbitt, in her reflections on the Lambeth Conference of 1998, shows how the Anglican Communion has been unable to avoid being gradually split: caught between increasing cultural diversity and the conflicts this produces on the one hand, and the need to provide coherence and identity on the other.

She notes how successive Lambeth conferences have moved sequentially from being grounded on traditional authority (i.e., the establishment of churches and provinces during the colonial era), to rational authority (which presupposes negotiation through representative constituencies for dominance over meeting outcomes), to (finally) negotiated authority (but which normally lacks the power to stem the momentum of change). She notes that these kinds of authority, when pursued through the four "instruments" of unity in the Anglican Communion, are usually capable of resolving deep disputes. They enable complex interaction and conversation, but they do not lead to clear and firm resolutions. Correspondingly, Nesbitt argues that a new fourth authoritative form has emerged within the Anglican Communion, which has in some senses been present from the very beginning, and is now tied up with the identity of Scripture. She writes of this authority:

> [It] could be used to countervail the relativism of cross-cultural alliances without affecting their strategic utility: symbolic authority. The symbol, as a locus of authority, has a tangible and timeless nature. Where the symbol is an authoritative part of the institutional milieu, either traditional or rational authority must acknowledge its legitimacy. . . . *Scripture* is [that] authoritative symbol. . . .[7]

Nesbitt points out that the symbolic authority of sacraments may create shared bonds and enhance communal cohesion, but they are normally unable to regulate or negotiate conflict. But in contrast,

> Scripture, when canonized as complete or absolute, becomes symbolic of a particular era or set of teachings and beliefs. However, unlike sacraments, the use of scripture as symbolic authority can be constructed and constituted according to selecting those aspects or passages that address an issue at hand. Furthermore, scripture as symbolic authority can be objectified or absolutized, which transcends cultural boundaries in a way that other forms of authority can less easily do. The appeal of scriptural literalism provides an objectification of authority that is independent of the influence or control of dominant perspectives, social locations, and circumstances. As symbolic authority, it can be leveraged against cultural dominance as well as provide common ground for cross-cultural alliances. . . .[8]

In other words, with Scripture raised almost to the level of apotheosis, a cross-cultural foundation for authority exists that can challenge the dominance of rational authority, which is normally associated with highly educated elite groups from the West or First World. Scripture, given symbolic authority, becomes an important tool in the hands of Southern (nonelite) Christians who are seeking to counterlegitimate more Conservative perspectives.

As Nesbitt notes, "Scriptural literalism as symbolic authority represents the easiest and most accessible form of counter-legitimation across educational or cross-cultural divides."[9] And as Lambeth Conferences, like the Anglican Communion itself, have become increasingly diverse in their cultural expression, symbolic authority has risen to the fore. So at present, and from one perspective, the only contender for being a focus of symbolic authority is the Bible, since cross-cultural negotiation only leads to sterile relativism. We should note that the only other alternative to the Bible—the Communion itself becoming or attaining the status of symbolic authority—has so far

---

7  Paula Nesbitt, *Religion and Social Policy* (Lanham, MD: AltaMira Press, 2001), p. 257.
8  *Ibid.*
9  *Ibid.*, pp. 257–258.

struggled to assert itself, mainly because the very resourcing of that requires a looser, more elastic view of truth-claims, and a necessary tolerance towards competing convictions.

This is a pity, because one of the chief virtues of living within a Communion is learning to be patient. Churches, each with their distinctive own intradenominational familial identity, all have to learn how to negotiate the differences they find within themselves. For some churches in recent history, the discovery of such differences—perhaps on matters of authority, praxis, or interpretation—has been too much to bear: lines have been drawn in the sand, with the sand itself serving only as a metaphor for the subsequent atomisation. Yet where some new churches, faced with internal disagreement, have quickly experienced fragmentation, most historic denominations have been reflexive enough to experience little more than a process of elastication: they have been stretched, but they have not broken. This is perhaps inevitable, when one considers the global nature of most mainstream historic denominations. Their very expanse will have involved a process of stretching (missiological, moral, conversational, hermeneutical, etc.), and this in turn has led directly to their (often inchoate) sense of accommodation. However, this process itself has led to two very different versions of the Communion and its future.

The first sees Anglicanism in concrete terms. The polity will be governed by law, and Scripture will be its ultimate arbiter. Here, Anglicanism will become a tightly defined denomination in which intradependence is carefully policed. Diversity of belief, behaviour, and practice will continue, but they will be subject to scrutiny and challenge. The second sees Anglicanism as a more reflexive polity; one that has a shape, but is able to stretch and accommodate considerable diversity. Here the polity will be governed by grace, not law, and the Communion itself will continue to operate as both a sign and instrument of unity. Anglicanism will continue to be a defined form of ecclesial polity, but one that tolerates and respects the differences it finds within itself.

Personally, I pray and hope for option two. But I also pray that I will not be divided from my sisters and brothers who favour the first option. I pray that in the midst of our common and diverse struggles, we will discover ourselves afresh in the learning church, within that community of peace we still know as the Anglican Communion. I believe that this may well stretch the Communion to its limits, and test its viability vigorously. But I believe the stretch will ultimately be worth it. For in reaching out just beyond ourselves, and moving outside our normal boundaries and comfort zones, God's own hand is already waiting to clasp at our feeble groping.

## Summary

If part of the problem that Anglicans are currently facing—namely a searching examination of our "deep identity" (manners, civility, tolerance, diversity, fluidity, etc.)—is itself being tested to the limits by cultural and theological diversity, then what might we say about our identity and ministry by way of a brief conclusion? The synergy between salt and motherhood, to which I alluded earlier, might now be said to come into its own. Both of those metaphors invite us to contemplate our future: how the process of attending to otherness is both necessary and enriching; that patient higgling and tholing is worth the effort; that the labour of being together might be worth more than the immediate and tangible fruits of clarity and certainty; and that what we offer and give to the world is costly and demanding; we nourish through our being and by our example.

Of course, both metaphors also suggest something else, namely that what is given in salting, fertilizing, or in mothering cannot guarantee any kind of uniform outcome. The cost of being a disciple is to recognize that although we may sow, tend, and water, it is God who gives the growth. And this growth is, at least in some ways, likely to be potentially problematic for any global denomination, because it invariably leads to difference and diversity. The Caribbean theologian Kortright Davis expresses this moment of epiphany simply enough:

> Western theologians are [now] attempting to educate themselves about the new theological surges emanating from the Third World. They have finally realized that there is no universal theology; that theological norms arise out of the context in which one is called to live out one's faith; that theology is therefore not culture free; that the foundations on which theological structures are built are actually not transferable from one context to another. Thus, although the Gospel remains the same from place to place, the means by which the Gospel is understood and articulated will differ considerably through circumstances no less valid and no less authentic.[10]

But to concretize this just a little more, let me offer three brief remarks. First, Anglicanism is something that is formed by worship, praying the Scriptures, and through an ecclesial practice that is, at one, local and catholic. A Communion is a complex body immersed in the complexity of the world, in which all seek to participate in God's purposes for a wide range of reasons. Anglicanism is, then, a kind of practical and mystical idea that embodies how people might be together. It is not a confessional church in which membership is conditional upon precise agreement with articles or statements. In spite of the internal difficulties that global Anglicanism encounters, its strength may still lie in its apparent weaknesses: its unity in its diversity; its coherence in its difference; its shape in its diffusiveness; its hope in a degree of faithful doubt; its energy in passionate coolness. It embodies "feint conviction"; it practices "truthful duplicity"; it is Protestant and Catholic; it is

---

10 Kortright Davis, *Emancipation Still Comin': Explorations in Carribbean Emancipatory Theology* (New York: Orbis Books, 1990), 70.

synodical and Episcopal; it allows for "troubled commitment"; or, as one commentator notes (Urban Holmes), it can hardly ever resist the pairing of two three-letter words: "Yes, but. . . ."

Second, maintaining unity in the midst of considerable cultural diversity will lie in developing our poise and capacity to hold together intensely held competing convictions. In the past, this rhetoric of "holding" has been treated with jocularity or even cynicism by the church and the public (including the media); it has been a kind of code for saying that no decisions can or will be made, (or the bishop doesn't like to make decisions, and prefers to sit on the fence). But increasingly, I think, the language and business of "holding" will need to come to the fore, and this work and vocation is very far from being vapid or neutral. "Holding" together intensely held competing convictions is, to my mind, one of the most demanding and costly tasks in episcopacy; a ministry of oversight that presides over conflicts of belief and interests. Under such conditions, the demand for a serious emotional and organizational intelligence (or wisdom) in dealing with passionately held beliefs is becoming increasingly vital.

Third, we may need to learn to celebrate the gift of our "undecidability" a little more. In being able to sustain a community of intense difference and competing convictions, we are actually offering a form of witness rather than a lack of unity. As the American theologian Urban Holmes notes, "I have never known two Episcopalians to agree totally . . . [but] the fact that we can admit our disagreements is indicative of our Anglican freedom to acknowledge the polymorphous nature of all human knowing—something that not every Christian body is comfortable admitting."[11] Holmes realizes that Anglicanism, although a system of a kind, is more identifiable through persons than articles of faith. It models itself through *examples* of faith. It is a "mode of making sense of the experience of God—a particular approach to the social and sacred construction of reality, and to the building of the world."[12] Anglicans occasionally write great theology, but they are better known for poetry, hymnody, liturgy, music, and spirituality. When we do get round to theology, we remain absorbed, interestingly, with the incarnation, ethics, and ecclesiology: all of these being person-centred and systematic attempts to concretize our witness within the world.

In summary, we can say that it is partly for this reason that our deep desire for Anglican comprehensiveness is so manifest. It is not the case, I think, that Anglican consciousness is essentially accommodating—especially in its more vapid forms. It is, rather, that comprehensiveness prioritizes conversation and quest over precision and absolute resolutions; at its best, Anglicanism is a community of being, love, thought, and worship, rather than being a definitive body that has achieved mutually agreeable confessional closure. In other words, we remain open because we see ourselves as incomplete; we are

---

11  Urban T. Holmes III, *What Is Anglicanism?* (New York: Morehouse Publishing, 1982), p. 31.
12  *Ibid.*, p. 29.

constantly caught between innovation and stability; the possibility of new patterns of being, and faithfulness to what has been revealed; between loyalty to what has gone before and still is, and what might or shall be.

Furthermore, the embodiment of this accommodation is, strangely, a person-centered ecclesial polity rather than being system driven. This is hardly surprising when one considers the historic Anglican affection for the doctrine of the incarnation: salvation comes through embodiment, example, sacrifice, and inclusiveness. Anglicans know—through their deep tacit knowledge and instinct, I think—that systems or formulae do not redeem us. Nor do they make our church. We're called, held, and saved by a person, and our polity seems to know that our being together (even with our differences) is primarily human and relational. This is why being together in some kind of "centre," where we can face one another with our different perspectives, and be in a place of conversation, is so vital for our future polity.

And this now means, of course, that the centre ground is becoming the *radical* ground: ironic and oxymoronic, I know—but holding to some kind of centre is, to a large extent, evolving into a task and role which makes the hardest demands upon those charged with oversight. All the more so, because as those who work and study in the field of international conflict resolution remind us, the most difficult and demanding battles are those which involve our own allies or close relationships: what one scholar rather tamely terms "cooperative disputes."

So our future life together as Anglicans is probably dependent on appreciating those implicit charisms and virtues that have shaped us for so long, and beginning to make them more explicit. And our having confidence in our undecidability and elasticity. Finally, in holding the church together, and keeping it open, remembering that we are first and foremost held by God in his open hands, who knows our weaknesses and differences only too well but will still cling to us, and not let us go. As we try to hold our people and ourselves together, so shall we be held. Urban Holmes ends his meditation on Anglican polity, written thirty years ago, with these words:

> [Our] course leads to living in the world as God sees the world. We can debate the trivial points, but the vision is largely clear. To love God is to relieve the burden of all who suffer. The rest is a question of tactics.[13]

---

13 Urban T. Holmes III, *The Future Shape of Ministry* (New York: Seabury Press, 1971), p. 245.

# 3

# ANGLICAN INTERPRETATIONS OF SCRIPTURE

## Can Scriptural Reasoning Provide a Way Forward?

*A. Katherine Grieb*

### Introduction: One Instance of the Current Impasse in the Anglican Communion

The Province of the Church of Uganda (Anglican), at its twentieth Provincial Assembly meeting held at Uganda Christian University, resolved on the concluding day of the Assembly (August 20, 2010) to suspend its participation in the Anglican Communion structures and its networks, the suspension to be reviewed at the end of four years, during which time the Province would focus on mission and ministry with likeminded Anglicans. The Province of Uganda's delegate to the Inter-Anglican Standing Commission on Unity, Faith, and Order reported that he would not be attending its next meeting, because "it is the considered view of the Province of the Church of Uganda that such meetings are a waste of valuable time and do not yield anything to help heal the broken and hurting Anglican Communion."[1] It seems probable that the Province of the Church of Uganda is reacting in part, at least, to the recent consecration of a partnered lesbian to the episcopate in The Episcopal Church, USA, just a few months before their Provincial Assembly. One definition of an "impasse" is "a deadlock" or "a predicament affording no obvious escape."[2] The purpose of this chapter is to explore possible causes of this particular impasse and to suggest a possible way forward.

---

1   Public Communication from Dr. Edison Muhindo Kalengyo to the members of IASCUFO, August 20, 2010.
2   *Webster's Ninth New Collegiate Dictionary* (Springfield, MA: Merriam-Webster, 1989). 603

## The Complexity of Anglican Interpretations of Scripture at Present

O God, by your providence the blood of the martyrs is the seed of the Church: Grant that we who remember before you the blessed martyrs of Uganda, may, like them, be steadfast in our faith in Jesus Christ, to whom they gave obedience, even to death, and by their sacrifice brought forth a plentiful harvest; through Jesus Christ our Lord, who lives and reigns with you and the Holy Spirit, one God, for ever and ever. Amen.

That Collect for the Feast of the Martyrs of Uganda, celebrated on June 3, remembers that on or about June 3, 1886, thirty-two young men were tortured in various horrible ways and then burned alive. If you were to look up this feast day in *Lesser Feasts and Fasts,* you would read that these "young men, pages of the court of King Mwanga of Buganda, were burned to death for their refusal to renounce Christianity."[3]

The impact of their deaths is also reported: "The example of these martyrs, who walked to their death singing hymns and praying for their enemies, so inspired many of the bystanders that they began to seek instruction from the remaining Christians."[4] Christianity had been introduced by a few Anglican and Roman Catholic missionaries nine years earlier (1877) under King Mutesa. His successor, King Mwanga, resolved to eradicate the faith and had martyred Bishop Hannington and his companions on October 29, 1885. But because these martyrs of Uganda in 1886 were indigenous Ugandans, they showed that Christianity was not a European-imposed religion; these were African Christians dying for their faith at the hands of an African king. Subsequent evangelization in Uganda was also carried out by Africans and Uganda is now the most Christian nation in Africa.[5]

A few years ago I visited the shrine of the martyrs in Uganda, or rather, the two shrines. Within a mile of each other are two shrines to the martyrs of Uganda, one Anglican and one Roman Catholic. Those young men who were undivided in their witness to the point of death were divided subsequently by the church. It was there in Uganda that I heard another version of the event found in *Lesser Feasts and Fasts:*[6] the memory of the Church of Uganda about these young men who became martyrs is that King Mwanga had tried to impose his sexual desires upon some of them. When they refused him because of their newly chosen Christianity, he responded by killing all the young men who were Christians. The story, as remembered by the Church of Uganda, makes no distinction between homosexuality and

---

3 *The Proper for the Lesser Feasts and Fasts* (New York: Church Hymnal Corporation, 1994), 258.
4 *Ibid.*
5 *Ibid.*
6 The historicity of the Ugandan version of the story is disputed by some historians.

pederasty[7] (it was young men and boys who were murdered by the tyrant) and it identifies Christianity and heterosexuality (the boys were not murdered for refusing sexual favors; they were martyred for their faith). In the mind of many in the Anglican Church of Uganda, the story of the founding of their church is the story of the triumph of brave young Christian martyrs over a tyrant who would impose homosexuality upon them against their religion.[8]

The first Anglican Ugandan clergy were ordained in 1893 and the Church of Uganda, Rwanda, and Burundi became an independent Province in 1961. In the 1970s the founding story of Uganda was repeated when a Muslim military dictatorship persecuted Christians and made thousands of new martyrs, both Anglican and Roman Catholic. It is reported that Idi Amin personally executed Janani Luwum, then archbishop of the Anglican Church of Uganda, whose courageous witness inspired Christians not only in Uganda, but around the world. The blood of the martyrs has indeed been the seed of the church in Uganda. In 1980, Burundi, Rwanda, and Zaire separated out into a new province and since then Uganda has grown from seventeen to twenty-seven dioceses, with a membership of eight million Anglicans in 1998[9] and certainly more than that by now.

Not many in the Episcopal Church in the United States of America would call twenty-one-year-old Matthew Shepard a "martyr": he did not die for his Christian faith, although he was a member of St. Mark's Episcopal Church in Caspar, Wyoming, before he entered the University of Wyoming near Laramie. His brutal death on the night of October 6, 1998, almost certainly because of his homosexuality (though these facts are also disputed), is more frequently labeled a hate crime.[10] And yet it seems to me that his death and the deaths of the Ugandan martyrs are related from a hermeneutical point of view.

For many in the Episcopal Church, the murder of Matthew Shepard reminded us of the deaths of Medgar Evers, Emmett Till, and hundreds of other young men who were beaten to death in the middle of the night and thrown into a river or lynched as a public example during the long centuries of slavery, rebellion, emancipation, reconstruction, depression, and finally

---

7  James Gaofenngwe Keetile mentions "the mistaken belief that homosexual men are always attracted to boys under the age of puberty" as one of the pejorative stereotypes about homosexuality prevalent in southern Africa. See his "A South African Reflection on the Issue of Homosexuality in the Anglican Communion," in *Anglicanism: A Global Communion*, ed. Andrew Wingate, Kevin Ward, Carrie Pemberton, Wilson Sitshebo (New York: Church Publishing, 1998), 207–10, esp. 208.

8  Keetile adds, "In some communities these prejudices [against homosexuality] are justified by pointing out that homosexuality as a topic is ideologically suspect, and is determined by Western societal concerns" (208). A Kenyan scholar described a woman in Kenya who said, in reaction to the news of the 2003 General Convention of The Episcopal Church USA, that homosexuality did not exist in her culture, that there was not even a word for it in her language. She concluded that it had been invented in Hollywood over the summer of 2003, and that TEC had decided to impose it upon the rest of the Anglican Communion because they could, the way U.S. leaders could impose economic and political policies on developing nations around the world.

9  *The Essential Guide to the Anglican Communion*, comp. James Rosenthal (Harrisburg, PA: Morehouse, 1998), 24.

10  See http://www.matthewshepard.org; http://en.wikipedia.org/wiki/Matthew_Shepard.

the civil rights movement. Their "offence" was being black in a culture that valued whiteness and feared blackness. Matthew Shepard's death prompted many people to link homophobia and racism in a way that they had not done before.

Those of us who watched translations of the Song of Songs 1:5 change from "I am very dark, but comely" in the RSV translation of 1952 to "I am black and beautiful" in the NRSV translation of 1989 have been reminded of the way that shifts in cultural perception inevitably affect the way Scripture is read. Studies of the way biblical texts were used by both abolitionists and slaveholders, and perceptions that the slaveholders had the stronger argument if the texts were simply weighed pro and con caused biblical scholars here to question the responsibility of the reader and the ethics of reading in biblical hermeneutics. Based on studies of the rich tradition of negro spirituals, many of us concluded that the illiterate slaves were better readers of the biblical text than were their masters who forbade them to learn to read but required them to go to church. They listened to the Pastoral Epistles, Colossians and Ephesians, which they were told were written by Paul (and many African Americans still hate Paul), but they "got" the deep logic of the exodus and the return from exile. They read themselves into the story typologically and trusted that the same Lord who delivered Daniel would deliver them as well.[11]

Growing awareness of the genocide against native Americans upon which the European colonization of our nation was founded, and the way that the biblical narratives of the exodus from Egypt and the conquest of Canaan had functioned typologically to warrant the extraction of the land from its inhabitants for the benefit of the churchgoing "elect" (including Anglicans) to whom it had been promised, warned white Americans precisely *not* to assume an easy identification between the biblical narrative and our own situation, or at least to question more carefully where we read ourselves into the story and what empowered us to do so. The social history of the United States and its impact upon biblical interpretation was being questioned by Anglicans here at precisely the same time that historical events in Uganda were reinforcing the founding narrative of the Anglican Church there.[12]

Not only founding narratives but current biblical reading practices help to shape precisely opposite hermeneutical strategies for Anglicans in Uganda and Anglican Episcopalians in the United States. The Revised Common Lectionary (RCL) that the General Convention (2006) mandated

---

11  George D. Armstrong, "The Christian Doctrine of Slavery: God's Work in God's Way," in *Religion in American History: A Reader*, ed. Jon Butler and Harry S. Stout (Oxford: Oxford University Press, 1998), 231–38. Religious support for slavery is outlined in Larry E. Tise, *Proslavery: A History of the Defense of Slavery in America, 1701–1840* (Athens: University of Georgia Press, 1987) and in Eugene Genovese and Elizabeth Fox-Genovese, "The Divine Sanction of Social Order: Religious Foundations of the Southern Slaveholders' World View," *Journal of the American Academy of Religion* 55 (1987): 211–33.

12  James H. Cone, *The Spirituals and the Blues: An Interpretation* (Maryknoll, NY: Orbis Books, 1972, 1991). Bruno Chenu, *The Trouble I've Seen: The Big Book of Negro Spirituals* (Valley Forge, PA: Judson Press, 2003).

for use beginning in Advent 2007 increases the number of readings from Deuterocanonical books of the Bible in an effort to bring the several denominations who share it closer together and also to more closely approximate the readings used by Roman Catholics who do not at present share it. But, as Griphus Gakuru has written, Uganda was evangelized by three evangelical missionary groups (the Church Missionary Society, the Africa Inland Mission, and the Rwanda Mission), so the Anglican Church of Uganda "does not recognize the Deuterocanonical books, which many call 'forbidden books.'" Gakuru was ordained in the Church of Uganda but received his doctorate in Old Testament studies from Cambridge. He adds, "It is apparent that elsewhere in the Anglican Communion these books are in liturgical use and this leaves many Ugandan Anglicans perplexed."[13]

The traditional African heritage concerning the authority of story and proverb complements the Anglican missionary heritage concerning the authority of Scripture. Though traditional African narrative is oral, and the Bible, though once oral, is now written, the two reinforce one another whenever the Bible is read aloud. As Gakuru comments, "The Scriptures are regarded as a deposit of authoritative and 'universally' recognized African-like sayings." Their status is proverbial. "The authoritative, universal and timeless nature of the African proverbial narrative has been bested in the Bible, summoning all people to listen and obey."[14]

The Church of Uganda expects every confirmed Anglican to read from the Bible every day, primarily in the context of the family. "For most families in rural areas, the Bible is the only book on the shelf. Its presence in every Anglican's home and the absence of other literature makes it the most read book."[15] Gakuru describes the prevailing hermeneutical methods as "allegorical" and "proverbial." He comments as follows about his home church:

> In this approach the word of God, which is believed to have intrinsic authority, becomes alive and extrinsically authoritative in a way today's Bible critic will not find it to be. This method also keeps the reading of the Bible simple and largely superficial. What the reader enters into is the world of the text itself, by-passing the historical and literary-critical concerns. And while this approach to the Bible makes it readable to all, it is incapable of yielding answers to complex and urgent questions, such as issues of justice, peace, and the integrity of creation.[16]

Gakuru has in mind the inability of the Church of Uganda "to condemn Obote's reign of murder and terror in the 1980s" and to respond "pastorally and sensitively to the AIDS epidemic." He notes that "using the allegorical

---

13  Griphus Gakuru, "An Anglican's View of the Bible in an East African Context," in *Anglicanism: A Global Communion*, 58–62, esp. 58.

14  *Ibid.*, 58.

15  *Ibid.*, 59.

16  *Ibid.*, 59.

method, some Church leaders frequently quoted Deuteronomy 28:22a, 27–28 (NRSV):

> The Lord will afflict you with consumption, fever, inflammation, with fiery heat and drought; The Lord will afflict you with the boils of Egypt, with ulcers, scurvy, and itch, of which you cannot be healed. The Lord will afflict you with madness, blindness, and confusion of mind.

Gakuru notes that some of these symptoms do resemble some of the symptoms of AIDS in its later stages.[17]

I would dispute Gakuru's forced choice between either reading the Bible critically or granting it extrinsic authority, but it is already significant that he makes that choice. Gakuru also calls our attention to the importance of the East Africa Revival, the great Anglican spiritual awakening that started in the 1930s with the Rwanda Mission: "Though originally not welcomed by the Church of Uganda, the Revival has by and large taken centre stage in Ugandan Anglican spirituality. What makes Ugandan Anglicanism unique is this Revival ingredient which has influenced the Anglican mode of talking about God and reading the Scriptures."[18]

Allan Anderson, director of the Centre for New Religious Movements, Selly Oaks Colleges, is a South African who was a member of a black-majority Pentecostal Church there. He claims that Anglicans in Africa are becoming Pentecostals. "Some are leaving the Anglican Communion, but many others remain committed Anglicans while practising a pentecostal form of Christianity," practicing traditional Anglicanism side by side with participation in pre-Christian African religious practices.[19] Such congregations stress the mighty power of God to save and heal, "To overcome all enemies and evils that threaten human life or vitality."[20] Anderson argues that as mission-founded churches, including Anglicanism, lose members to Pentecostalism, one way these churches are coping is to incorporate more elements of Pentecostal piety into their Anglicanism.

Gakuru describes in some detail the Revival pattern of taking one verse or phrase from the Bible as a theme for the day, so that a series of speakers give personal testimony in the light of that bit of text. This doubles the oral and proverbial African tradition with that of the Bible's authority read in an oracular way. It is the Revival Anglicans who have spearheaded mission and

---

17  *Ibid.*, 62, n7. See Grant LeMarquand's report of a panel discussion on the plight of so-called "dis-abled" people in Limuru, Kenya, in June 2003, "Biblical Reflections on a Panel Discussion on 'Disability,'" in *Theological Education in Contemporary Africa*, ed. Grant LeMarquand and Joseph D. Galgalo (Eldoret, Kenya: Zapf Chancery, 2004), 211–17. See also his "'And the Rulers of the Nations Shall Bring Their Treasures into It': A Review of Biblical Exegesis in Africa," *Anglican Theological Review* 88, no. 2 (2006): 243–55.

18  *Ibid.*, 60.

19  Allan Anderson, "African Anglicans and/or Pentecostals: Why So Many African Anglicans Become Pentecostals or Combine Their Anglicanism with Pentecostalism," in *Anglicanism: A Global Communion*, 34–39, esp. 34.

20  *Ibid.*, 36.

evangelism in Uganda; they are responsible for the large increase of numbers in the Church of Uganda, especially during the Decade of Evangelism in the 1990s.[21]

Gakuru writes from the perspective of a priest of the Church of Uganda who has done his doctoral studies in Great Britain and now resides there. It is important also to hear the voices of members of the Church of Uganda who are not biblical scholars and not presently living elsewhere in the Communion. For that reason, I include here a lengthy quotation from Beatrice Musindi, a Ugandan woman, taken from Alistair Redfern's *Being Anglican,* comparing the Church of England to the Church of Uganda. We could substitute "the Episcopal Church" every time she says "Church of England" and get the desired effect:

> Christians in Uganda are not afraid to speak up about their faith with whoever they come across. In other words, faith to them is never a private affair. They usually tell others of what the Lord has done in their lives and encourage them to have the same experience. Certainly, they are quite sure of and genuinely "proud" of their faith. In Britain however, the reverse is evident. People are not open about their faith. A lot of people do not want to be too involved with church matters. An hour for a Sunday service is all they can afford to give. Time is far too precious to be wasted on "religious" things. What is disheartening is that some clergy are not inclined to the active spreading of the gospel.
>
> Many of the Anglican churches in Uganda function primarily with lay leadership. This, I believe, is among the things English Anglicanism needs to learn from other parts of the Anglican Communion. . . . In Uganda, like anywhere else in the Anglican Communion, worship is vital. Ugandan Christians worship God with their whole being. They clap hands, dance, use local musical instruments and encourage spontaneity. On the contrary, worship in English Anglicanism lacks joy. It is so "serious" and glum. No doubt a lot of young people do not find church exciting at all. . . . The Anglican Church in Uganda takes spirituality very seriously. The influence of elements of the revival is still evident in church today. Personal testimony, or witness and fellowship are emphasised. In England, people tend to take everything for granted and do not spend much time in prayer (for provision of daily needs), while in Uganda there is a greater dependence on God to provide and protect. Uganda Christians always pray before a journey, for example; a Christian in England just hops in the car and drives off.
>
> In addition, enphasis is put on Bible study. This enhances a personal knowledge of the word of God as well as fostering communal life. Certainly family life is elevated. . . . Interestingly, a lot of Christians

---

21 Gakuru, "An Anglican's View of the Bible in an East African Context," in *Anglicanism: A Global Communion,* 60.

in England have little expectation that God will act, so they feel they have to do it themselves as individuals. This has caused a lot of isolation instead of God's children living as the family of God.[22]

In this chapter, I am not interested in any attempt to refute her perceptions, but rather to understand them and to notice how far apart she thinks we Anglicans are in our convictions and our practices.

Also important are the dynamics of postcolonialism and population demographics. As Philip Jenkins has argued, the average Anglican in the world today is a poor woman located in Africa.[23] In parts of the Anglican Communion where the Anglican Church has been established or has functioned as a national church, it will probably be assumed that the Episcopal Church, for example, endorses the economic and military policies of the United States government and agencies like the World Bank that have destabilized national economies. Postcolonial critique need not limit itself to the colonizing nation but extends its critique to colonizing practices and mentalities wherever they are located. Kevin Ward, in an article on the history of the Anglican Communion, writes as follows:

> President Yoweri Museveni of Uganda (who happens to be an Anglican) was interviewed at the time of the Edinburgh Commonwealth Conference in October 1997. Asked about the role of Britain and the English language in the new Commonwealth, he replied with a parable: "When we were fighting in the bush, the regime in power got arms from abroad. Our job as guerrillas was simply to wait and grab those arms. Similarly, you came to our countries and we captured your language. Here I am speaking to you in your own tribal language.[24]

Given the phenomenal growth of Anglicanism in Uganda and in many other parts of Africa, and the strong postcolonial hermeneutic in place there, there is little reason to think that traditional Church of England–related ways of being the Anglican Church will be other than that which has been "captured" and is ripe for revival and transformation along very different lines.

For this reason, Rowan Greer's magisterial study of Anglican approaches to Scripture from the Reformation to the present;[25] John Booty's thoughtful essay on tradition, traditions, and the present global crisis;[26] and other such

---

22 Beatrice N. Musindi, quoted in Alistair Redfern's *Being Anglican* (London: Darton, Longman and Todd, 2000), 130–31.

23 Philip Jenkins, "Liberating Word: The Power of the Bible in the Global South," *The Christian Century*, July 22, 2006, 22–27. See his *The New Faces of Christianity: Believing the Bible in the Global South* (Oxford: Oxford University Press, 2006).

24 Quoted in Kevin Ward, "The Development of Anglicanism as a Global Communion," in *Anglicanism: A Global Communion*, 13–21, esp. 13.

25 Rowan A. Greer, *Anglican Approaches to Scripture: From the Reformation to the Present* (New York: Crossroad, 2006).

26 John Booty, "Tradition, Traditions and the Present Global Crisis," in *No Easy Peace: Liberating Anglicanism, A Collection of Essays in Memory of William John Wolf*, ed. Carter Heyward and Sue Phillips (Lanham, MD: University Press of America, 1992), 73–90.

attempts to identify an "Anglican hermeneutic" or a set of best practices in the Anglican tradition[27] may provide interesting distillations of what *has* been characteristic of Anglicanism over the last several centuries and what *may still be* characteristic of Anglicanism in certain parts of the Anglican Communion that remain more tightly linked to that tradition. But it will either be largely irrelevant to or will function negatively, as that which is to be avoided, in the fastest growing parts of the Anglican Communion. Rowan Greer's comment is instructive:

> One of my prejudices, to put it that way, is a bemusement about the controversies that now divide Christians in general and Anglicans in particular. It is hard for me to think of any time in history when people have not cried out that the church is in danger, but it does not seem to me that God is in danger. The present controversies have resulted in an unfortunate polarization that makes it difficult to engage in argumentation, passionate or dispassionate. . . . For these reasons I do not regard what I have tried to do in what follows as having any direct bearing upon present controversies save for insisting that we need to be somewhat more cautious in appealing to the "right" view of Scripture.[28]

Appealing to the "right" view of Scripture is precisely the point of much of the condemnation of the Episcopal Church and others by the Anglican Church of Uganda and others.[29] The question of what is Anglican interpretation has become much more complex than it was during the period of history about which Rowan Greer wrote. The hermeneutical assumptions, our reading practices, and the founding and foundational experiences which shape our hermeneutical perspectives are so disparate that the Anglican Church of Uganda and the Episcopal Church of the United States of America might almost be different denominations.

## Might the Scriptural Reasoning Project Provide a Way Forward Together?

If the hermeneutical differences among us are as great as I think they are, could the approach of scriptural reasoning that has been modeled by Jewish, Christian, and Muslim scholars assist us in hearing one another and learning to reason about the Bible together? The second half of this chapter will explore

---

27 See my own much more modest attempt to outline such an approach in "An Anglican Interpretation of Scripture," *The Record* 104, no. 1 (Spring 2007): 8–9.

28 Greer, *Anglican Approaches to Scripture*, xxv–xxvi.

29 But not all of it. I would be the first to regret that the Episcopal Church did not inform itself better about the recent histories and postcolonial perspectives of much of the rest of the Anglican Communion before acting in General Convention in 2003. I would also note that if a full and frank discussion of this difficult issue had been allowed, and indeed required beforehand in theAnglican Communion, the perceived offence might not have been so great. These are speculative matters about which one can only guess. It is also possible that the outcome would have been exactly the same even if all the "right steps" had been taken.

that question. Perhaps an approach to Scripture that has been able to deepen mutual respect and form collegiality among scholarly practitioners of the three Abrahamic religions, with all the difficult politics and perennial disputes about past history (much of it violent) among them, could also work to deepen *koinonia* and to strengthen the "bonds of affection" that are the essence of the Anglican Communion.

The Scriptural Reasoning project grew out of "textual reasoning" conversations between a group of academic Jewish text scholars (primarily TaNaK and Talmud) and philosophers and theologians who wanted to engage in interdisciplnary studies. They met regularly to study biblical and rabbinical texts in conversation with Western philosophy, particularly with Jewish philosophers who had themselves attempted to reason philosophically about traditional Jewish texts. They used the term "textual reasoning" to identify the two sides of the conversation: "The interpretation of traditional texts and the practices of philosophical and theological reasoning."[30] They discovered that Judaism after the Tremendum needed to return to and reengage both its scriptures and their traditions of interpretation, on the one hand, and, on the other hand, to engage with others who were also wrestling with the meaning of their faiths in postmodernity, especially Christians and Muslims.

Ford explains that Peter Ochs (who had known Hans Frei and George Lindbeck at Yale) had studied their postcritical, "postliberal" hermeneutics. What they had learned from the Christian theologian Karl Barth resonated with the approach of the Jewish thinker Franz Rosenzweig. A conversation group formed around Peter Ochs at Drew University in the late 1980s and early 1990s that also included Christians and Muslims.[31] When the textual reasoning group began in 1991, cochaired by Peter Ochs and David Novak, it already had the potential for Abrahamic conversation built into it.

When David Ford and Daniel Hardy (both Anglican theologians) began to attend meetings of the textual reasoning group at the American Academy of Religion (AAR) in the early 1990s, "scriptural reasoning" was born. Jewish-Christian at first, it expanded to become Jewish-Christian-Muslim in the late 1990s. A small group agreed to meet regularly every summer for a few days of intense scriptural study; a larger group met twice a year at Cambridge and at the AAR to discuss various aspects of scriptural reasoning. Ford describes four key strands of the project: 1) Jewish textual reasoning as already described; 2) Christian postliberal text interpretation associated with Karl Barth as interpreted by Hans Frei at Yale; 3) a range of less text-centered Christian philosophies and theologies, both Protestant and Catholic; and 4) Muslim concern simultaneously for the Qur'an and for Islam in relation to

---

30 David F. Ford, "An Interfaith Wisdom: Scriptural Reasoning Between Jews, Christians, and Muslims," in *The Promise of Scriptural Reasoning*, ed. David F. Ford and C. C. Pecknold (Oxford: Blackwell Publishing, 2006), 1–22, esp. 3.
31 *Ibid.*, 3.

Western modernity, especially in questions of the natural and human sciences and technology.[32]

Since then, partly as a result of others having attended scriptural reasoning groups and of the group's publication of some of its findings, several more scriptural reasoning projects have begun in various places, such as the Abrahamic Roundtable of which I am now a member in the Diocese of Washington. My own first encounter with textual reasoning was at a late-night session at an AAR/SBL meeting sometime in the 1990s that centered on the Akedah, the Binding of Isaac. I believe only Jewish scholars and a few extra observers like myself were present. Curious about the term "textual reasoning," I was strongly impressed by a group that would begin its meeting at 10 or 11 pm and run several hours after that. They had to be seriously engaged with the biblical text to make that kind of commitment.

David Ford describes scriptural reasoning as "a wisdom-seeking engagement with Jewish, Christian, and Muslim scriptures." Scriptural reasoning begins with the assumption that "each tradition's scripture is at the heart of its identity." They are "formative for understanding God and God's purposes; for prayer, worship, and liturgy; for normative teaching; for imagination and ethos; and so on."[33] Scriptural reasoning assumes that all religions meet new situations that challenge them to develop over time; discussion of any important development will inevitably involve appeals to scripture. "Many of the bitterest disputes within and between all three faiths centre on appeals to scripture. So an attempt to deal with the core identity of any of the three will inevitably involve its scripture."[34]

Scriptural reasoning, like other postliberal projects, places a strong emphasis on "traditions" and with "generating the right kinds of tension"[35] between and within traditions. Its task is to improve "the quality of our disagreements" rather than to avoid conflict, "increase tolerance, or secure consensus."[36] Ben Quash, author of one of the essays in the volume, notes four "marks" of scriptural reasoning: "particularity, provisionality, sociality, and readiness for surprise." People who engage in scriptural reasoning "must speak from a particular place, from their own distinctive viewpoint, from the specificity of their traditions and with a heightened pitch of attention to their particular texts in relation to others. This particularity enables attentiveness to texts, time, contingency, and the provisionality of the practice, as well as the sociality it enables when particularity is so valued."[37]

As Pecknold expresses it, "being generous and critically receptive, even vulnerable, to one another's judgments has been a key part of the ethos of

---

32 Ibid., 4.
33 Ibid., 1.
34 Ibid.
35 Alasdair MacIntyre, After Virtue: A Study in Moral Theory (Notre Dame: University of Notre Dame Press, 1981), 160.
36 C. C. Pecknold, "Editorial Preface: The Promise of Scriptural Reasoning," The Promise of Scriptural Reasoning, vii.
37 Ibid., viii.

engagement in scriptural reasoning" because such an ethos "enables each participant to discern the genuine otherness of their [own] tradition." The experience of reading one's own tradition with others who serve Abraham's God makes strange the text, the tradition of interpretation, and even the God who stands behind the text. Each such engagement implies "a theological recognition that each tradition-constituted, tension-dwelling identity remains open to, and hopes to be formed by, God's judgment."[38]

One of the aspects of scriptural reasoning that I find most attractive and most potentially promising for the family argument that we are having within the Anglican Communion at the present time is the notion that each participant brings to the table not only "his or her scripture, a much-studied and much-loved book" but also what Aref Nayed has called our "internal libraries" consisting of everything people have learned, "not only through tradition-specific activity in study, prayer, worship and experience" but also "through their academic studies and from their cultural locations, their arts, their economic, political, and social contexts."[39] They offer one another "hospitality" where "each is host to the others and guest to the others as each welcomes the others to their 'home' scripture and its traditions of interpretation."[40] Such hospitality requires shared practices, and David Ford lists a few of these in the form of maxims that I will summarize briefly here:

- acknowledge the sacredness of the others' scriptures to them, since each group believes that their scripture is in some sense from God and that their group is interpreting it in the presence of God.

- the aim is not consensus: that may happen, but a recognition of deep differences is more likely.

- do not fear argument, as one intellectually honest way of responding to differences—part of mutual hospitality is learning how to argue in courtesy and truth.

- allow time to read and to reread, to entertain many questions and possibilities, to let the texts unfold within their own traditions of interpretation, to stick with a text without premature resolution of its difficulties, to sound its depths.

- read and interpret with a view to the fulfillment of God's purpose of peace among all and be open to mutual hospitality turning into friendship.[41]

As I write these words, I am mindful that it took seventeen years of long, patient, and sometimes difficult conversation among representatives

---

38 *Ibid.*, x–xi.
39 Ford, "An Interfaith Wisdom," *The Promise of Scriptural Reasoning.* 4–5.
40 *Ibid.*, 5.
41 *Ibid.*, 5–6.

of Anglicanism and Greek Orthodoxy to get to the point of publishing the Cyprus Statement of 2006.[42] It is one of the fullest statements of an ecclesiology of communion we have and it tackles some of the most difficult questions about the naming of God, the uses of metaphorical and iconic language to represent God, and the possibility of women representing God to the church and the church to God as priests or bishops. It is also precisely at this point that I begin to doubt the effectivenss of a process like scriptural reasoning or that engaged in by the Anglicans and Orthodox for our present conflicted situation.[43]

The very mixed blessing of the Internet and the World Wide Web means that communication can travel instantly around the global Anglican Communion. It also means that a local statement becomes both public and not retrievable at the same time it is spoken. An announcement over the Internet becomes effective seconds later and may have repercussions of which its author never dreamed. Older communication patterns were more conducive to dialogue. A letter conceived in anger or sorrow could be written and not sent after a good night's sleep; a letter of resignation or insult could be "misplaced" on the receiving end and never effectively arrive; there was room for the art of diplomacy; there was time to think before responding; there were opportunities to consult with cooler heads and with others whose interests might be directly touched. All of these evaporate when someone in an important ecclesiastical role issues an opinion or perhaps an ultimatum to someone else or to some other part of the Anglican Communion.

Moreover, all the things that work towards stereotyping and the reinforcing of ill-conceived prejudices are magnified by the impersonality of the medium. In today's texting world, it is impossible to see the tears on the page or to imagine the trembling hand behind the jagged letters. There is no tone of voice or facial expression that might help either the sender, who could, having seen the reaction, back off; or the receiver, who could, having seen the demeanor, interpret the words more wisely.

The message is sent and something about this medium also seems to imply that an answer must be forthcoming at once. We rob ourselves of the time we humans need to think complex things through.

All this is complicated by the role of the news media and their preference for sound bytes that tend toward confrontation and resist either resolution of differences or postponement of a discussion until a later time. Until we can structure our conversations in ways that will do justice to the complexity

---

42 *The Church of the Triune God: The Cyprus Agreed Statement of the International Commission for Anglican-Orthodox Theological Dialogue 2006* (London: Anglican Communion Office, 2006).

43 Not because either group of churches would be unable or unwilling to engage in the constructive listening process involved in meeting one another at a table where the biblical texts that seem to come between us are studied together. Nor do I doubt the gracious presence of the Lord who has promised to be there wherever two or three are gathered together seeking wisdom from God through the biblical texts. Judaism knows this presence as the Shekinah of God who presides over the study of Torah, while Christianity invites the Holy Spirit of God to lead us into deeper truth. My concern, rather, is that we will be undone by modernity before we can even begin a postliberal conversation.

of the issues and that honor the depth of our conversation partners and the importance of the experiences that have shaped their hermeneutical assumptions, I fear that we will not really engage one another at all.

The church ought to be one of the few places where it is still possible to have a good argument. We need to find a way that the Anglican Church in Uganda can be invited to tell the stories of its martyrs and be heard as it rightfully wants to resist the imposition of homosexuality upon its youth by a foreign power. We need to find a way that representatives of that church and others with similar experiences can ask questions of the Episcopal Church, the Anglican Church of Canada, and the Church of England. We also need to find a way for these churches to bear witness to the Church of Uganda and others to the grace of God given to their gay and lesbian members who have been patiently waiting for recognition of their humanity and full membership in the church for a very long time.

For all of these reasons, I believe the Anglican Communion initiatives stemming from the Lambeth Conference of 2008 that involve increased work on the processes of biblical interpretation and hearing one another's stories; increased attention to the Listening Process by which the experience of gay and lesbian Christians around the Anglican Communion is recognized; increased attention to the office of bishop and to collegiality and wisdom-seeking among bishops; and increased attention to the welfare of institutions of theological education around the Communion, especially where that involves sending students to some other part of the world and/or bringing them to Canterbury. All these plans are, it seems to me, exactly the right sort of things we need in order to deepen our own conversation about scriptural reasoning. May God give us enough time to practice hospitality within our tradition by hearing one another's experiences and by listening to one another's arguments that we may walk forward together into an Anglican Communion that at present we cannot even imagine.

# 4

# AN ECUMENICAL CONJECTURE ON MISSION

## Bonds and Limits of Anglican Communion[1]

*Tom Hughson*

Whether or not ecumenism proceeds as one organized movement with a decided goal or is an association of many heterogenous initiatives with a common hope for deepening unity without a defined goal is an interesting question. It involves whether or not there is but one method par excellence for ecumenism, the method of dialogue that is the calling card of the ecumenical movement. To ask the question is to suggest a possibility that the ecumenical movement is one but not the only basic model of ecumenism. Another might be ecumenism as a loose association of hopeful conversations, official contacts, and cooperations, and local practices with a general direction and more than one main method, not excluding dialogue. That would be my inclination at the present. The method of dialogue at any of its levels and in every mode excels in preserving ecclesial identities while allowing for common exploration of past sources of division and from time to time an unsuspected new consensus that moves churches bilaterally beyond some particular past point of division.

But may there not be other basic models and methods? One would be a model of "receptive ecumenism" pioneered at the University of Durham with a method that invites each church to ask itself what it so far has learned and in the near future hopes to learn from other churches. Another approach, and I hesitate to name so small and personal a model, has a starting point in the blessing of friendship and whose inner logic is one of looking to the good of each other's churches as communities whose members one wishes well. The logic of friendship differs from a logic flowing from a primary preoccupation

---

1 The 2010 meeting of the Society for the Study of Anglicanism featured presentations by Robert Hughes and Rob Slocum. A panel responded. These remarks were prepared as notes for one panelist's response and were subsequently edited.

with resolving particular points of division, or with step-by-step progress to a future unity, or with recollecting lessons learned. At least the little model of friendship serves to express something of how I as a Roman Catholic value participation in the Society for the Study of Anglicanism.

I receive the papers by Robert Hughes and Rob Slocum with agreement, certainly with the theme of preserving unity in the Anglican Communion. My response consists in offering an additional perspective from which to think about the matter. In regard to the topic of the bonds and limits of Anglican Communion, and not presuming to speak with special expertise on the official Anglican/Catholic relationship, I'll offer a Catholic's conjecture of a formal sort. That is, I don't have a developed position at stake in addressing the bonds and limits of Anglican Communion, and so I will be guided by the logic of the ecclesial subject matter to raise an open and not merely rhetorical question. The question: is not church mission an important vantage point from which to think about the bonds and limits of communion? The question pertains to every church or ecclesial movement and not only the Anglican Communion. That is, it springs from the nature of the church and not the particulars of present tribulation. What is the nature of the church? An answer would have to be comprehensive of a number of models, not least communion, and that exceeds the scope of this reflection. But one salient dimension of the church that belongs to its innermost constitution is mission. Ecclesiological consensus, represented by the World Council of Churches document on *The Nature and Purpose of the Church* and the Church of England 2004 report, *Mission-Shaped Church*, holds that the church—the whole of divided Christianity and each church and ecclesial movement within it—is missionary by nature.

In a bit more detail, what does that ecclesiological consensus say? The church is missionary by Trinitarian nature, not only by dominical commission, not primarily because of ecclesiastical decisions to send missionaries, and not because some Christians are inspired to volunteer for foreign missions. "By nature" means in virtue of being constituted by and sustained in the Trinity, not as if the church like other created entities had an internal nature of its own with relative autonomy in its operation. Not only have the missions of Son and Spirit (themselves identical to the inner Trinitarian processions with the addition of a temporal effect, according to Aquinas) instituted the church. Unlike a Deist idea of divine creation as God's clockwork left to its own devices, the *missio Dei* from the Father through the Son and in the Spirit structures and continually sustains the church's very specific kind of mysterious existence which becomes most active and manifest in the Eucharist.

"Missionary" means the church does not exist simply and solely for the salvation of members, as if Matthew 28 were adding the extra task of going to all nations to a church already finished in its founding. Rather, both Jesus' commission in Matthew 28 and Pentecost in Acts 2 reveal that mission belongs to the founding. Trinitarian *missio Dei* constitutes the church as a participant in Christ's mission and not only a hearer of Christ's word. Christ and the Holy Spirit co-constitute the church. Pentecost impels the gathered but incapacitated disciples not only further into the saving message but also into the ongoing and outgoing mission of Christ. Only with participation in Christ's mission do the church and discipleship become complete in their basic orientations. "Missionary by nature" means as well that all baptized and confirmed followers of Christ enter into the church's mission, not just some who are designated and dedicated missionaries.

As a result some say the church does not have a mission, mission has a church. That is true but oversimplifies the mystery of the church. As a Trinitarian communion for the glory of God, the church has an aspect of being an end in itself and not only a divinely instituted social instrument for mission. That is, nourished by Word and Sacrament, the community as a whole along with baptized and confirmed disciples as individuals have an intrinsic finality through faith in Christ to communion (*koinonia*) with Father, Son, and Holy Spirit, to liturgical and personal worship, to fellowship, and to service. But discipleship at the same time and by reason of baptism, confirmation, and Eucharist has a finality toward mission as action in history.

Picking up where David J. Bosch's magisterial *Transforming Mission: Paradigm Shifts in Theology of Mission* (1991) left off, Stephen Bevans and Roger Schroeder in *Constants in Context: A Theology of Mission for Today* (2004) have clarified the variety of ways in which the missionary nature of the church is being appropriated, understood, and enacted as mission, often simultaneously in the same church. Three distinct yet complementary concepts of mission are: 1) mission as *missio Dei* drawing people into *koinoina* and then directed through the missions of Christ and the Holy Spirit to gaining all humanity for the life of Trinitarian communion; 2) mission as joining with Jesus' historically initiated mission of establishing the kingdom of God, including contemporary work for justice, peace, and the integrity of creation; 3) mission as proclaiming the unique and universal saving power of the Lord Jesus Christ to all nations and those who may have forgotten.

Moreover, mission as action in history, though oriented beyond present church membership, cannot be split away from the internal, pastoral ministry of Word and Sacrament. In *Church Drawing Near: Spirituality and Mission in a Post-Christian Culture* (2003), Paul Avis made the intriguing proposal that Word and Sacrament are also the primary mode of mission in a secular, post-Christian culture insofar as pastoral ministry and ordained ministers are able to respect and cultivate an openness to the sacred that is dormant and occasionally awake in nonchurchgoers. In any case, mission cannot be separated from pastoral ministry when it comes to the place of Word and Sacrament in witnessing to and communicating the gospel from one generation to the next in catechesis, baptism, and celebration of the Eucharist. Liturgy too has a missional aspect.

Whether church mission is understood along the lines of *missio Dei*, building the kingdom of God, or proclaiming the Word, or more likely a combination of all three with one or the other taking the lead in different circumstances, the church has an inbuilt direction beyond itself into historical praxis that gives witness (*marturia*) and leads to communication (*euanggelizthai*) of the gospel to those who have not heard it. A secondary form of witness and evangelization, re-evangelization, brings the gospel again to those in cultures where Christianity has flourished in the past but who have not heard it presented effectively in their lifetime or having heard have since drifted away. Again, the church is missionary by nature. Anglican mission, then, offers no merely incidental or adventitious basis from which to consider the bonds, substance, and bounds of Anglican communion. To the contrary, taking account of the church's inner momentum toward mission can claim to be a perspective indispensable to pondering the Anglican Communion in any aspect, including the bonds and limits of communion.

And yet even the briefest reprise of an ecclesiological consensus on the missionary nature of the church has to include admission that the consensus does not extend to how that nature is to be enacted in contemporary circumstances. There is no assurance about the praxis of mission today as there was in the early church and through the whole modern period of Christendom, not least the nineteenth century. But many are the new conditions that have altered the foundation, motives, aims, and nature of church mission in the twentieth century. Already in 1991 Bosch had pointed to the following modern factors creating a crisis of mission—1) secularization; 2) de-Christianization of formerly Christian countries and cultures; 3) religious pluralism in most places; 4) Western guilt from colonialism; 5) the spectacle of rich Christians in a poor world; 6) the decentering of Western churches. More recently, British authors Richard Bauckham, David Smith, and Paul Avis have added postmodernism to the factors. I would like to place one more on the list, the most obvious of conditions—division within Christianity. All of these together have resulted in the praxis of evangelization, mission, or witness coming to seem unsettled and obscure at the same time that consensus has emerged on the missionary nature of the church.

Nonetheless and granted the missionary nature of the church, how can reflection move pastorally and theologically back from the outward-oriented missionary nature and activities of the Anglican Communion to the internal bonds and bounds of Anglican Communion? The path is not obvious and has foggy stretches, but there are points of reference. One is the link between church unity and church mission. A second is the history, not historiography, of mission in Anglicanism. A third is what may be called a missionary imagination that works from mission and its success or not to questions of membership, identity, and fidelity. A fourth concerns implications in models of mission.

The first point of reference is the familiar truth that what fosters structural unity within and among churches improves conditions for credible evangelization. Appreciating that divided churches impaired the credibility of the gospel led to the 1910 World Mission Conference in Edinburgh, credited with launching the modern ecumenical movement, notably with attention to missionary practice. Paul's letter to the Ephesians affirmed one Lord, one faith, one Spirit, and one baptism. But witness and evangelization already have appeared in a deficient light when their proximate, enveloping actuality is rival kerygmas from opposed churches. That situation puts before prospective Christians a bewildering variety of competing baptisms. Consequently, whatever is church-dividing is mission-dividing, and dividing mission impairs the credibility and effectiveness of evangelization. The obvious implication for Anglican Communion has to do with every effort to keep the various parts of the Communion from splintering into parts that will inevitably end up as rival evangelizers. At the least does not the centenary of Edinburgh encourage the thought that the archbishop of Canterbury's efforts to prevent structural division serve not only the internal bonds of fellowship but the cause of the gospel to be conveyed by Anglican mission?

At the same time World Wars I and II showed the fragility and naïveté of aspiration for Christian unity transcending national borders that does not involve transformation of local contexts. Does not this fragility of Edinburgh's 1910 hope indicate that in matters of unity and diversity, analyses continually have to take critical account of the possible influence from one sort or another of nationalism, including U.S. nationalism in the form of cultural predispositions preformed as are most things religious in the U.S. by a Calvinist, free-church heritage? Would not conscientious, faith-based self-criticism of nationalist impulses and meanings be a spiritual discipline essential to sustaining Anglican community in faith (or communion in other churches too)?

A second point of reference is the history, not historiography, of Anglican mission. Although with laudable postcolonial perspective, much modern historiography pillories all modern missionary activity as the velvet glove on the iron fist of Western imperialism. But the actual history more than likely is less clear-cut, more mixed. Are there not some inspiring examples in the records of Anglican and Episcopal missionary work of men and women who genuinely asserted and proceeded from the primacy and supremacy of Christ, gospel, church, and faith over sponsoring nation and empire? Postcolonial critiques of the association of missionaries with imperial plans, measures, resources, and protection are important and to the point, of course, and not to be dismissed. But sometimes sweeping, generic criticisms may overlook the self-transcending labors of particular people and efforts. Are some leading figures in the history of Anglican mission people to look to as a precedent and resource in thinking about the bonds and limits of communion? Did not they too have to struggle with Anglican bonds and limits, though in a different historical horizon but still in the face of differences latterly identified as cultural but that in first encounter often bore religious meanings?

Third, another point of reference in thinking from mission to the bonds and limits of communion is a missionary imagination about church unity evident in Acts 15:1–35. The proto-council of apostles and leaders furnishes an instance of missionary imagination. Those assembled in Jerusalem were well aware that some followers of Christ with a Pharisee background were teaching and advocating that Gentile converts must undergo circumcision and observe the whole Mosaic law. They knew this was neither a uniform practice in spreading the gospel nor a unanimous conviction among the apostles. The difference in their midst portended conflict and division. So they listened to Paul and Barnabas describe their work among Gentiles blessed by signs and wonders. The assembly, while not mandating the same way of life for Jewish followers of Christ, accepted a solution for Gentiles brought forward by Peter and James in favor of Paul and Barnabas's approach. They decided against a demand for Gentile circumcision and took a position favoring limited observance of Mosaic law by Gentile members of Christ's followers. The decision did not state that the Gentile solution replaced Jewish Christian practices of circumcision and substantial observance of Mosaic Law. Interestingly, there seems to have been no thought given to the possibility that some such as Paul, Barnabas, Peter, and James would hive off from the rest in order to carry out their inspired practice, their fidelity to Christ, and their witness to the gospel.

Still, what may be most instructive consists first in the whole framing of the problem in reference to communicating the gospel way of life to prospective and new members of the church. And second in prayerful searching for how God was acting on behalf of increasing the reach of the gospel of Christ. The controversy arose from, was deliberated on, and resolved with attention to God's lead in communicating to and instructing new Christians. Could it be that recasting the problems of communion from the perspective of prospective and the newest of Anglicans would bring to light possibilities hidden to preoccupation with church order and one or two moral issues? What else might be learned from Acts?

Possibly this. The council in Jerusalem exemplified accurate, careful communication and deliberation on public matters of the gospel. Contrary, controversial opinions were circulating in local churches, so Paul and Barnabas went in person to meet with the apostles in Jerusalem. They dropped whatever they were otherwise doing, and did not write a letter as Paul so often did in his ministry with various churches across the Mediterranean world. The meeting itself seems to have had a structure, with a process of discussion, then deliberation, then a decision. One cannot help but think of the importance of the Lambeth Conferences in this regard. Does a missionary imagination such as Luke's in Acts 15:1–35 and in the apostles at the council have exemplary value in confronting issues that test the bonds and limits of Anglican Communion?

A fourth point of reference in thinking back from mission to bonds and limits in communion concerns models of mission. Because no consensus holds sway on what missionary practice ought to be, theologians have proposed various models. Among them are the model of "prophetic witness" developed by Scottish theologian David Smith in *Mission After Christendom* (2003) and a model of "prophetic dialogue" explained by Bevans and Schroeder in *Constants in Context*. Both books acknowledge a debt to Bosch's *Transforming Mission* and its ecumenical paradigm. Both Smith and Bevans/Schroeder point to a post-Christendom relationship between Christianity of the North and the South as the defining feature of mission today. They both look ahead to a future significantly shaped by the fact that Pentecostals are the fastest-growing sector of Christianity, and both books see the question of how Christianity relates to non-Christian religions as the crucial axis of inquiry for mission. Just to take one of the models, does the model of "prophetic witness" contain implications for the bonds and limits of Anglican Communion, particularly communion between Canterbury and Africa?

Smith's "prophetic witness" relies on a premise that Western empire-building begun in fifteenth- and sixteenth-century voyages of discovery has reached a zenith in economic globalization, à la Negri and Hardt's idea in *Empire* of a free-floating empire of capitalism. Communications technology and economic transactions have spread the idea of the primacy of economic life and the market. The result has been increased divisions between and inequalities within societies, not a homogenous overcoming of gross inequalities. Further, Smith's premise notes that from the sixteenth to the twentieth century, missionaries coming from Christendom, excepting a few, coincided with, accompanied, and to some degree colluded in empire-building. Failures in respect to human and cultural dignity under Christendom requires of churches after Christendom that mission involve a critical perspective on the new reality of economic globalization. Smith proposes a "prophetic witness" in which a church and congregations confess in theory and practice, in the spirit of Paul and the book of Revelation and as a critique of power, that Jesus is Lord, meaning that no one and nothing else is ultimate sovereign.

According to Smith, mission places European and North American churches before this question: Can they listen to Christians in India, Africa, and Asia and accept Jesus as a crucified Lord in suffering people and churches? Can they read the book of Revelation to renew Christian imagination by purging it of propaganda disseminated by the Empire of global capital, and thereby teach the subversive alterity of faith? Then mission comes to mean not sending missionaries, but above all an ecclesial and personal commitment to spreading the gospel and the kingdom of God. In Smith's global view, Northern Christianity, wealthy and childless, may come to seem a biblical Babylon to a resurgent Islam, Hinduism, and Christianity in the poor, charismatic, and conservative South. In that situation, churches and mission in the North have the task, Smith suggests, of positioning themselves within the North as a bridge to a South they seek to listen to and a North they seek to help understand the South.

Does Smith's model of mission as prophetic witness offer any pathways of reflection into matters of diversity, fidelity, and conscience in contemporary Anglicanism? Would not Anglican churches, and not just in England, in Europe, North America, and Australia resituate some of the tension and conflict with churches in various African nations if churches in nations sponsoring and most benefiting from globalization took up a project along lines proposed by Smith? Ideally Smith's critical prophetic witness would be qualified and inflected by John Atherton's more analytic and redemptive perspective in *Transfiguring Capitalism: An Enquiry in Religion and Global Change* (2008). Would not such a mission go some distance toward demonstrating the real consequences of adopting a postcolonial approach to mission and to the South that affirmed a solidarity in common commitment to and labor for the well-being of all Anglicans and Africans?

In conclusion, the foregoing conjecture on the advantage of mission as a starting point in pondering the bonds and limits of Anglican Communion has been almost entirely formal in the sense of generically Christian and based on the missionary nature of the church rather than on Anglican ecclesiology and self-understanding. Much of the conjecture could be applied *mutatis mutandis* to other churches and ecclesial movements. The purpose was only to ask a question, leaving answers to those with standing as Anglicans and more knowledgeable than I about discussions and positions on the bonds and limits of Anglican Communion.

# 5

# A SPIRITUALITY OF RECONCILIATION FOR THE ANGLICAN COMMUNION

*Philip Sheldrake*

I am challenged by your Society to reflect on the subject of reconciliation—not least at this painful time for the Anglican tradition. By way of personal introduction, I am a professor of theology at the University of Durham, England, and have been closely involved since the mid-1980s on both sides of the Atlantic in the development of Christian spirituality as an interdisciplinary field of study. I was an ordained member of the Jesuit religious order for many years but am now married. I remain a Roman Catholic yet a friendly outsider/ insider who has been engaged with Roman Catholic–Anglican reconciliation for most of my life. This commitment originated in my childhood as I negotiated the complexities and challenges of mixed parenthood and an unusually ecumenical education at a time of sharp religious divisions.

This chapter is really a manifesto for keeping faith with reconciliation at a time when siren voices suggest that a quick divorce in the Anglican Communion would now be less painful, more honest, and less distracting. Yet I continue to believe that the complicated theme of "reconciliation" is vital for the inner life of the church precisely because it is also vital for Christian mission at the start of the twenty-first century.

Apart from my own mixed origins, why do I believe that reconciliation is so important humanly speaking as well as to what it means to be Christian? This is a theological question for, as the South African theologian John de Gruchy suggests in his Cambridge Hulsean Lectures (in his case, strongly influenced by Karl Barth), the doctrine of reconciliation is "the inspiration and focus of all doctrines of the Christian faith."[1] Over the years, I became convinced of two things. First, consciously chosen separations and divisions in Christianity offer no real answer to the human problem of difference and

---

1    John de Gruchy, *Reconciliation: Restoring Justice* (London: SCM, 2002), 44.

disagreement. The separation of the Reformation did not produce some form of pure religion. For centuries it sadly encouraged a dangerous misbelief that what is contrary to the Spirit of God lies outside ourselves in a demonised or caricatured "other." St Augustine's *City of God*, often cited as *the* manifesto of Christian separation from a sinful world, is no such thing. The tares and the wheat, as Augustine made clear, are destined to remain together until the end of time because we have no means of recognising infallibly which is which. Indeed, we know in our more honest moments that the tares and wheat actually coexist within each one of us.

Second, the world desperately needs to hear a new word about reconciliation. Christianity is called to speak that word—precisely and unashamedly a theological-spiritual one. But a divided church has little credibility in preaching reconciliation to a divided world. There is no point in *speaking* reconciliation unless we are seen to commit ourselves to trying to live it in all its pain, ambiguity, and incompleteness. This is a counterintuitive message in our contemporary cultures so driven by the search for quick solutions, simple answers, and clear distinctions.

## The Words We Use

The words we use are important. So what does reconciliation imply? Is it the same as political models of conflict resolution? Several words are often treated as interchangeable: reconciliation, conciliation, and accommodation. Conciliation is associated with pacifying or placating. This lowers the temperature but does not necessarily promote deep change. Many peace negotiations conciliate but fail to transform people at the deepest level. Accommodation or tolerance enables the establishment of pragmatic arrangements, compromise, and a kind of parallelism. However, reconciliation goes far deeper. Interestingly the *Oxford English Dictionary* defines reconciliation not merely as the restoration of harmony but also as "the reconsecration of desecrated places." If you like, all those people whose lives are marginalised by what we do or say are "desecrated places" because their unique value and identity as images of God is denied.

## Costly Reconciliation

Reconciliation, first of all, implies a complex balance between structural change and spiritual harmony.[2] Secondly, the *process* of reconciliation is evolutionary and it is important to avoid quick or "cheap reconciliation." Conflict

---

2 On the process of reconciliation, the works of the Catholic theologian at Chicago, Robert J. Schreiter, are especially insightful. See his *The Ministry of Reconciliation: Spirituality and Strategies* (Maryknoll, NY: Orbis Books, 1998) and *Reconciliation: Mission and Ministry in a Changing Social Order* (Cambridge MA: Boston Theological Institute Series, 2000).

always involves issues of power and so reconciliation implies a gradual redistribution of power in ways that cannot just be theoretical.

This leads me to the critical thought that reconciliation can only be *between equals.* Therefore it results from *making equal space for "the other."* This is different from tolerance, which can simply promote a series of parallel, boundaried spaces. It is a structural issue, but it is also a psychological, theological, and spiritual issue. At the heart of reconciliation lies an initial belief that everyone is diminished by the situation we seek to change. So the quest is for new ways of collaboration that will empower everyone. The foundation must be a genuine attempt to avoid closed judgments.

Reconciliation demands that everyone has to modify their view of the world and to risk the way they identify themselves in that people so often identify themselves "over against" something or another group. We tend to handle "otherness" by different forms of exclusion. So for example:

- We demonise—we fear those who are "other" and seek to eliminate them. Our desire is that they surrender or die away.

- We colonise—we think of others as inferior and to be pitied. They become objects of our charity or our bullying.

- We generalise—we take care not to see others as individuals, but only as "a type." Our desire is to keep control of the situation and not have to deal with the challenge of personal encounter.

- We trivialise—we ignore disturbing differences and domesticate the strangeness by allowing some to become honorary members of our club. Our desire is not to be challenged by their presence but affirmed as good people for allowing them to join us.

- We homogenise—we say there's no real difference at all. In a well-meaning way, we make premature pleas for tolerance and closure.

- We ignore—we simply make the other disappear by not acknowledging them at all.

## Fear and Loathing

The major problem with conflict and reconciliation is not moral or intellectual disagreement but fear and loathing. Fear is one of the most powerful currents in our contemporary world. On-going religious or ethnic divisions, as well as the "war on terror," suggest how fear and its close associate anger shape our responses and cripple our ability to respond effectively to the deeper needs of fellow humans. The overwhelming imperative then becomes the satisfaction of emotional needs posed by fear and anger. We tend to rush towards emotionally satisfying but actually superficial actions—we detain dissidents, expel illegals, or marginalise certain voices without addressing the deeper challenges. Fear and anger are among the greatest spiritual blocks to effective discernment and choices.

Fear and unacknowledged anger tend to promote evasion, hiding, and paralysis, and work in three ways:

1. Both provide a narrative structure to answer the question of why we are in a mess. This needs a clear plot and a plausible cast of goodies and baddies. The story line must be big enough to provide a convincing description of our fear which usually means that the threat is greatly inflated. Such narratives offer emotional reassurance on several levels. They affirm that it's understandable that we are afraid; that we are on the side of good versus evil; that good (meaning our perception of good) will prevail.

2. Both respond to our desire for uncompromising clarity. When we are fearful, we want to know who's on our own side and we want loyalty to be unconditional rather than complex. Everyone is assigned a label. Nowadays, there is a growing tendency to escape into wilful ignorance—people do not *want* to understand if understanding is not straightforward.

3. Both prompt a desire to bond with the apparently like-minded. There is much talk of standing together and shared values. But the quest for meaningful identity in such an oversimple sense is always at risk of buckling under the weight of too many hidden contradictions.

## Spaces

Reconciliation involves "making space" for the other. We have to make historical space for the other. Our histories are never neutral or value free. All histories are partial in that they are built on what is included and excluded. A critical question for every human community, including the church, is what kind of historical sense do we foster? Humans tend to rehearse a particular version of history as the justification for maintaining barriers of separation. We therefore need a new history that enables the emergence of a shared narrative to embrace everyone rather than a select few. A new history liberates everyone, albeit painfully, by relativising cherished myths and allowing the recovery of forgotten voices.

Every conflict leaves scars. A process of reconciliation must make space for *memory*. The Latin word *memoria* has connotations of mindfulness. This relates both to attentiveness (to people, contexts, and my own reality) and to "embracing the whole" as opposed to a comfortable and comforting forgetfulness. Reconciliation does not mean forgetting but re-membering in a new way, in a new context where we learn how to remember *together* rather than continue to trade memories in the same way we trade blows. Space for memory enables communities as a whole to begin to come to terms with the truth of the past. To have to speak and to have to listen is profoundly trans-forming. Reconciliation involves the healing of memories, particularly of belittlement, rejection, and denial. Part of a process of healing is to realise the incompleteness of any one story when isolated from the other stories. So a space for memory also implicitly celebrates diversity.

Both the space for history and for memory essentially involve a process of growing into a shared vocabulary which ultimately cannot be imposed but which arises from shared life and shared experience.

## The Process of Reconciliation

Reconciliation is an extended process, not a single moment. In the "foundation stage," there will be *remembering*—all that has been forgotten or buried—and *recognition*—the need to begin with truth-telling. In any movement of recon-ciliation, everyone needs to acknowledge guilt, selfish attitudes, and rigidity. We have to learn, patiently and slowly, how to listen to "the other" and to hear their pain. Listening, correct hearing separated from our deep-felt "right-ness" or prejudiced assumptions, is a tough discipline (what has been called a "hermeneutic of generosity"). In the end, spiritual reconciliation requires everyone to recognise the frailty of their own movement towards conversion and an acceptance of redemption. There is no one, no party, no group that is not bound to face the evil within—hatred or destructive anger. There is a pro-found connection between reconciliation and spiritual healing.

In the "transformation stage" we must be prepared to accept some loss and grief. There needs to be *repentance*: of attitudes and actions; *refusal*: to participate in structures of exclusion; and *restitution*: the ethical dimension of reconciliation. Because words and actions of rejection have desecrated the image of God in others, reconciliation demands repentance for attitudes and actions that promote the exclusion or diminishment of "the other." There needs to be a serious commitment not to participate in behaviour that vio-lates the other. There is always restitution after repentance. This may involve a variety of things that are not material such as the restoration to others of their identity.

In a "readjustment stage" there needs to be *reconstruction*—of a vision and of new forms of community; *empowerment*—of all those involved (although some may paradoxically experience it initially as loss); *forgive-ness*—the mutuality that is a long-term hope. True reconciliation is bound up with the reconstruction of a quite different world of discourse and practice. This consists of identifying what is needed, creating a vision, and making that vision a concrete reality.

- All must commit themselves to learning how to listen and to hear without distortion.

- All must make the effort to enter other peoples' experience and to leave their own aside.

- All must try to see themselves through others' eyes.

- There must be a willingness, with the help of others, to disentangle truth and falsehood in one's own perceptions and in what we assert. What really needs reconciling? The presenting issues are not necessarily the whole of the truth.

- We must be prepared to enter into a process of genuine discernment of what needs to be retained and what must be put aside.

- And, above all, we must accept the equal seriousness of the other.

## Christian Reconciliation

There are specifically Christian characteristics to reconciliation—it is not simply a political or psychological word with some incidental theological-spiritual gloss. Protestantism tends to emphasise reconciliation between God and humanity as a result of the Cross (cf. Rom. 5:6–11), and Catholicism tends to emphasise how the love of God poured out upon us as a result of the divine-human reconciliation creates a new humanity in which the walls of division between people are broken down (cf. 2 Cor. 5:17–20; 6:1). In practice, both dimensions need to be held in tension. Interhuman reconciliation is not simply a matter of giving each person their due but is really to give God *God's* due, by building a world and a church that God's all-embracing forgiveness demands.

## Catholicity and God

A key word is "catholicity," which fundamentally relates to the nature of God.[3] In other words, while catholicity is something we affirm about the church, how we describe the Christian community is rooted in a particular under-standing of God. We may suggest that only God is "catholic" in the sense that God alone embraces the "mystery of the whole." What do we learn about cath-olicity if we begin with God? This is a complex question that I can only touch upon briefly. God-as-Trinity speaks of a *koinonia* or communion of mutually coinherent relationships in which the unique personhood of each is substanti-ated in mutuality.

Early Christian writers developed the theme that the *koinonia* between believers brought about by *koinonia* with Christ in the Spirit is a sharing in the very life of God. So in 1 Cor. 1:9, Paul expresses gratitude for the Corinthians having been called by God into *koinonia* with Christ—often translated as "fellowship" but actually participation in the life of Christ. In 2

---

3  For a fuller development of what follows, see Philip Sheldrake, "Practising Catholic 'Place'—The Eucharist," *Horizons: The Journal of the College Theology Society* 28, no. 2 (Fall 2001): 163–82.

Cor. 13:13, *koinonia* is a gift from the Spirit so that our life in common derives fully from our *koinonia* with Christ in the Spirit.

In other words, the implication of a Trinitarian God for human existence is that God's presence-as-action is the source of, and goal of, the inner dynamism of every person. God may be said to ground every person in their particularity. However, the "catholicity" of God-as-Trinity not only grounds but also expands the inner dynamism of each person. If the Trinity expresses an understanding of God in which the particularity of the divine persons is shaped by mutual communion, the Trinitarian presence within each of us underpins the uniqueness of particular identity, yet at the same time subverts self-enclosure by orientating us to what is other. We might say that a Trinitarian anthropology suggests an inherently transgressive rather than individualised and interiorised understanding of identity.[4] Catholicity implies giving space to everything and everyone that God gives space to.

## Catholic People?

Catholicity concerns how we "perform" Christianity. It implies "telling the whole truth," or "telling the whole story." A vital part of that telling, beyond mere exposition or proclamation, consists in living what might be called Catholic *lives*—that is, the way in which the fullness of God revealed in Jesus Christ is brought to realisation in us. The catholicity of God-as-Trinity is expressed in time and space through the Incarnation. Thus, the heart of the catholicity of the church, without which the concept remains insubstantial, is the person of Jesus Christ. In Christ, "the whole fullness of deity dwells bodily, and you have come to fullness in him who is the head of every ruler and authority" (Col. 2:9–10). And "From his fullness we have all received, grace upon grace" (John 1:16). So the first element of catholicity is a *participation in God's catholicity in and through following Jesus Christ.*

We struggle with how "the whole story of Jesus Christ" is to be embodied in the particularities of our lives. I suggest that there are five key elements. First, becoming catholic is not at the most fundamental level a matter of affirming certain beliefs in an objective, intellectual sense, although belief is certainly part of the equation. It is a matter of *living* Christ—in other words, a matter of how Jesus Christ's story of God-become-flesh, of the proclamation of God's kingdom, of the triumph of God-given life over suffering and death, is made present here and now in the lives of those who belong to the community of people bearing Christ's name. So a second fundamental element of catholicity is *being part of a people,* a universality of particularities, expressing unity in diversity by journeying with a family of faith that has integrity and yet is open to a God who cannot be confined within its boundaries. Third, this also implies *living in the stream of a tradition* in the sense

---

4   See Colin Gunton, *The Promise of Trinitarian Theology* (Edinburgh: T & T Clark, 1997), 112ff; and also his *The One, The Three and The Many* (Cambridge: Cambridge University Press 1995), 164.

of practising a way of life shaped by the complex history of this community. The two foundational sacraments of Baptism and Eucharist concern, among other things, incorporation into this people and this tradition. Becoming catholic concerns the process by which we enter into an Easter narrative of human existence.

Living within the "whole story" of Jesus Christ's story also implies coming to grips with the full story of our human existence and so a fourth element of catholicity is that it is *all-embracing*. However, to "tell the whole story" is also to speak of human incompleteness, failure, false aspirations—the ambiguity of lives that are both graced and sinful. The sacraments of Baptism and Eucharist speak of this as well, and of the process of reordering the disordered, healing what is broken, reconciling what is alienated. Seeking catholicity implies an ability to acknowledge a whole life in which human imperfection paradoxically becomes a foundation for receptive learning.

The notion of "becoming" is a crucial fifth element of catholicity. Becoming catholic is a process of hope, the hope of transformation that never ends within time and space. The whole truth of Jesus Christ is always *in process of being* realised in us. So a fundamental quality of this vision of becoming is expectancy. Expectancy implies knowing that there is more and becoming ever more receptive to "the more" that we need. This receptivity is perhaps most sharply expressed in and through our engagement with people and communities that are unlike, other, strange, unnerving, and even distasteful. By acknowledging that God, and the space God enables, is the fundamental reference point, Catholicity is, in this sense, self-subverting in that it undermines its own tendency to become fixed and to proclaim its own self-sufficiency. This is perhaps counterintuitive.

The process of spiritual transformation that we name as holiness is precisely a movement of being drawn ever more deeply into the depths of God. This is inevitably, at the same time, a process of stepping into a way of unknowing or dispossession. Only by an engagement with the depths of God (who alone expresses "the mystery of the whole") may we ourselves be drawn into the mystery of catholicity. As St. John of the Cross expressed it in his great text of mystical theology, *The Ascent of Mount Carmel,* to arrive at the mystery of the whole or to possess "all" is not a matter of the accumulation of, or possession of, more and more particular things, even truths. On the contrary, he emphasised a paradoxical theology of *dispossession* whereby the desire for more and more "things" (that by definition are less than "everything"—*todo* in John of the Cross's language) is stripped away in favour of union with the "all" that is God alone.

> To reach satisfaction in all
>
> desire its possession in nothing.
>
> To come to possess all
>
> desire the possession of nothing.

To arrive at being all

desire to be nothing.

To come to the knowledge of all

desire the knowledge of nothing.

To come to the pleasure you have not

you must go by a way in which you enjoy not.

To come to the knowledge you have not

you must go by a way in which you know not.

To come to the possession you have not

you must go by a way in which you possess not.

To come to be what you are not

you must go by a way in which you are not.[5]

## Becoming Catholic—The Demands of Hospitality

The quest for "the mystery of the whole" necessarily involves a sense that we continually need to receive. A receptive catholicity is not simply a matter of structure or doctrine but is an encounter of people—a "conversation" between two horizons that inevitably changes both. The very process of engagement and conversation is revelatory in that we come to realise that God speaks not simply in *my* tradition (intratextuality) but in the very conversation and interaction that we share (intertextuality).

An important concept is "hospitality." Interestingly, the emphasis in both Hebrew and Christian scriptures is most strongly on hospitality to the stranger. In the gospels, Jesus is frequently portrayed as the wanderer without a home (e.g., Matt. 8:20) or dependent on the hospitality of others (e.g., Lk. 9:58) or, in the Gospel of John, as the stranger in our midst (e.g., John 8:14, 25ff). Hospitality to the stranger is presented as the vision of the Kingdom of God—and, indeed, has a bearing on our eternal destiny in Matthew 25. What is critical is that hospitality is not the same as assimilation of what is "other" into me. It is not a question of finding the last piece of the jigsaw that completes my lack or our need—that ultimately gives me only what in a sense already belongs to me. Hospitality concerns the reception of what is strange and what *remains* strange or at least "other."

The Christian narrative of redemption describes the nature and destiny, alienation and glory, of humanity. It speaks of *alienation* (from God, from each other, and from creation) but also of how God overcomes alienation, redeeming humanity from the bondage of sin. The Cross offers a new concept of reconciling love that risks everything, accepts death and rejection, and

---

5    John of the Cross, *The Ascent of Mount Carmel*, Book 1, Chapter 13, 11. Translation from the Spanish in K. Kavanaugh, ed., *John of the Cross: Selected Writings* (New York: Paulist Press, 1987).

so enables the transformation of the unjust. The paradox is that it is out of weakness, rejection, and death that new life comes. Yet reconciliation is not yet experienced in its completeness—for the evil of human division remains a reality. For now there is an assurance, a confident hope that God will finally establish justice and peace. The church, as prolongation of the mission of God, is called to embody proleptically the narrative of reconciliation.

In addition, "reconciliation" in Paul speaks of the one who is offended (God) as the one who takes the initiative in seeking an end to hostility. This contrasts with human assumptions that reconciliation should be initiated by "the offender" and that an acknowledgment of guilt is an absolute *precondition* of reconciliation. Christian reconciliation also challenges the notion that difference should be viewed purely as part of the human predicament. Trinitarian theology speaks powerfully of a God in whom difference is the foundation of existence. Ephesians also relates reconciliation to participation in the church. A new covenant community becomes the carrier of the vision of a new humanity in which Jew and Gentile are reconciled as members of one body. What is it to "be in common"? Communion—existing in common—is more than a statement or definition but equally it is also more than sentiment. It is, at its heart, an expression of the life of the Trinity. Precisely by struggling to *live this life* we share in God's work of reconciliation. Linking together Ephesians 2:11–22 with Galatians 3:23–29, Paul witnesses to a radical transformation of human status. The walls of enmity are broken down; those far off, even the enemy, are made near.

## A Spirituality of Reconciliation: The Rule of St. Benedict

In the final part of this chapter, I want to turn our attention to two elements of what might be called a "spirituality of reconciliation." I want to refer first to the Rule of St. Benedict—and as a corollary to the Book of Common Prayer—and second to reflect on the Eucharist.

The impact of a Benedictine ethos on the origins of the Anglican tradition, particularly the emphasis on prayer and life "in common" in the 1552 *Book of Common Prayer* (BCP) and its later revisions, alongside more classical Reformation sensibilities, hardly needs rehearsing. Benedictine spirituality has a great deal to offer as well in terms of the Christian vocation of reconciliation. I simply want to mention two words.

First, the opening word of the Rule is "Listen!"—*Obsculta!* This sets the tone for the whole Rule and its approach to the Christian life. At the heart of reconciliation lies a commitment to listening. For this we need to learn silence, to cultivate attentiveness so that we become capable of receiving what we are not and what we do not have. Silence counteracts a rush to angry judgment and destructive words. The Rule, of course, is full of scriptural quotations and resonances, and a broad analysis of the Bible shows that "listening" or "hearing" takes precedence over activity. Listening, attentiveness, is associated with true wisdom and this, in turn, is connected not only with our relationship to God but to the notion of obedience—obedience to the Rule but, by implication, to the community and its life together. Listen contemplatively to your brethren for here God speaks; here is the "school of the Lord's service," a school of discernment and wisdom. Listening implies giving oneself wholeheartedly rather than conditionally to the common enterprise. And, finally, listening implies being silent in order to learn or to be taught. Chapter 6, On Silence, *De Taciturnitate*, reinforces this. The word used is *taciturnitas* not *silentium*. That is, not merely being quiet but being sparing in what one asserts; being the opposite of domineering; keeping one's mouth firmly closed so that the evil thoughts or the lies in our hearts may not issue forth. In this discipline, we may slowly be converted to a gracious heart.

The spiritual quality of "silence" is closely related to reconciliation because it implies a refusal to engage in polemic which the Rule considers unchristian. The Rule goes on to say that acceptable speech in community should always be (a) modest and (b) reasonable. Other monastic texts talk of "silence" as a necessary preparation for speech that is meaningful rather than ill-thought out. Do not rush to speak, the texts say, or to assert. Above all, avoid speaking out of anger. But of course there is a wrong kind of silence—refraining from speaking out. By implication all *good* speech is informed by contemplation—of God first but also, by extension, in a contemplative attentiveness to the other. The point is that silence and listening are part of the process of good communication.

Reconciliation is closely related to another key Christian virtue taught by the Rule—hospitality. RSB 53: *Omnes supervenientes hospites tamquam Christus suscipiantur.* All are to be received as Christ. But notice, the Rule goes on "for he himself will say, I was the stranger and you took me in." Christ is the stranger. This implies a deeper theology of hospitality than merely giving food and board to a passing visitor. Commentators have always noted the *omnes*—an inclusiveness linked particularly to *strangeness*, or we might say "otherness," in contrast to those who are "like us." *Supervenientes,* "those who arrive," underlines the point even more strongly. It literally means those who "turn up out of the blue." However, this is not a question merely of those who did not warn us they were coming but those *who are a surprise to us* in a deeper sense. Close to the surface of the text is the understanding that Christian disciples are not to be choosey about whom they keep company with. And *hospites* is a nicely ambiguous word that can be translated as "stranger" as well as "guest." The former sense is reinforced by the reference to Matthew 25:35. Finally, *suscipiantur* literally means "to be received," but its deeper sense is to be *cherished*—the stranger turns into someone who, while different, we learn to value as closely as if they were one of our own.

## The Book of Common Prayer

Turning to Thomas Cranmer's appropriation of the common prayer of the Rule in the BCP, this is more than a matter of liturgical practice. It encapsulates a liturgical ecclesiology. The church is not defined by statement or confession (an idealised ecclesiology or ecclesiology "from above") but by practice "from below." Liturgy is the *locus theologicus* of the church. The church is, as it were, practised into existence. Thus, a liturgical ecclesiology is 1) a dynamic process rather than static; 2) derived from the totality of the community and its practice; 3) by the grace of God; 4) never complete. First, prayer is fundamentally "in common." When we listen *together*, for example, we hear the scriptures in a particular way. This operates on more than one level. On the literal level, we hear prayers and scriptures spoken or sung aloud thousands of times in the course of a lifetime and thereby, on a deep level, acquire a tacit understanding that every reading is always qualified and supplemented by other moments, other readings. Equally, we are drawn into a wider flow of times and places—a history of readings—and realise that way that our own readings of Scripture, tradition, and worship are in so many ways the products of our social and cultural environments. But that is not to invalidate them. It is the only way to *start* reading but it can never be where the reading *ends*. Isolated reading—or reading and praying only in the company of the like-minded—to read and to pray inadequately.

But the spiritual tradition of the BCP also embraces the notion that what is defined by and created in common prayer is a mysterious "common house" that transcends easy definition. No, the "common house" of the BCP is the place where all manner and condition of people rub shoulders, often uncomfortably, yet in that "to and fro" of spiritual negotiation find a common home. Note too the obvious point that the BCP offers a tradition of common *prayer* as the source of life together. In such a life of prayer we also learn that God's movement takes place in the *loci communes,* the ordinary places of this world—in the nitty-gritty, not in a purified or protected realm set apart.

This is also manifested in the seventeenth-century spirituality of George Herbert, so imbued with the spirit of the BCP, where in his famous poem, "Prayer," one of the metaphors is "Heaven in ordinary." This expresses the mundane transfigured by the radiance of divine glory. But it implies more. An "ordinary" in Herbert's time was also a menu of cheap food, or the part of the inn where this was served, or the common and disreputable people who ate such fare. "Heaven in ordinary"! This notion of God's revelation among people of ill repute echoes another of Herbert's poems, "Redemption," where God, the "rich Lord," is sought by the speaker yet not found as expected "in great resorts" but shockingly among the "ragged noise and mirth" of the kind of disreputable people one might encounter in a cheap bar. Such a contrast to the notion of Anglican spirituality as genteel and respectable!

## The Eucharist as Place of Reconciliation

The heart of a Christian spirituality of reconciliation is the Eucharist. The catholicity of God is sacramentally expressed explicitly in the *koinonia* of believers filled with the Spirit of the Risen Jesus and shaped by the Eucharist. The Eucharist is not simply a practice of piety but the enactment of the special identity of Christian community. As such it is an *ethical* practice, although not simply in the superficial sense that it provides an opportunity for a didactic form of moral formation.[6] It seems to me that the link between ethics and the Eucharist is intrinsic rather than extrinsic.[7] Ethics embodies a way of being in the world that is appropriated and sustained fundamentally in worship, especially the Eucharist. Conversely, the Eucharistic enactment of catholicity necessarily opens the community to appropriate ways of living in the world.

A sacramental perspective on reality demands a reordering of the existential situation in which we exist. To live sacramentally involves setting aside a damaged condition in favour of something that is offered to us by grace for "where we habitually are is not, after all, a neutral place but a place of loss and need" which needs to be transformed.[8] Part of this damaged reality consists of our flawed identities—whether these suggest that we are people of power or diminish us as people of no worth. The transforming dynamic of the Eucharist demands that the presumed identity of everyone be radically reconstructed. This necessitates honest recognition, painful dispossession, and fearless surrender as a precondition of reconciliation.

To enter the "space" of the Eucharist implies a radical transformation of human "location" such that it is no longer to be centred on the individual ego or on safe gatherings of the like-minded but discovered in being a-person-for-others. Every time the Eucharist is celebrated, all those who commit themselves to cross the boundaries of fear, of prejudice, and of injustice in a prophetic embrace of other people, without exception, in whom we are challenged to discover the "real presence" of an incarnate God.

Reconciled in the Eucharist, the members of the Body of Christ are called to be servants of reconciliation among men and women and witnesses of the joy of resurrection. As Jesus went out to publicans and sinners and had table-fellowship with them during his earthly ministry, so Christians are called in the Eucharist to be in solidarity with the outcast and to become signs of the love of Christ who lived and sacrificed himself for all and now gives himself in the Eucharist.[9]

The Eucharist is very much a "landscape of memory"—including

---

6   The link between the enactment of identity and the ethical nature of the Eucharist is discussed by the moral theologian, the late William Spohn, *Go and Do Likewise: Jesus and Ethics* (New York: Continuum, 1999), 175–84.

7   On this point, see Donald E. Saliers, "Liturgy and Ethics: Some New Beginnings," in *Introduction to Christian Ethics: A Reader,* ed. Ronald Hamel and Kenneth Himes, (New York: Paulist Press, 1989), 175–86.

8   Rowan Williams, *On Christian Theology* (Oxford: Blackwell, 2000), 209–10.

9   *Baptism, Eucharist and Ministry,* Faith and Order Paper 111 (Geneva: World Council of Churches, 1982), para 24.

ambiguous or conflicting memories. Beyond the immediate participants, there are wider and deeper narrative currents in all Eucharistic celebrations. The central narrative, that is, the revelation of God's salvation in Jesus Christ, enables all human stories to have an equal place and yet at the same time reconfigures them. The Eucharistic narrative makes space for a new history that tells a different human story beyond the selectivity of tribalism or sectarianism. It invites us to undertake the radical business of creating human solidarity and changing the status quo. The Eucharist, despite our various human attempts to regulate and control it, engages a power beyond the ritual enactments themselves to offer an entry point for the oppressed, the marginalised, and the excluded.

The Eucharistic action, according to its own inner logic, speaks radically of Catholic "space" in the world of space and time. There is, therefore, a perpetual and uncomfortable tension between the sacramental practice of God's reconciliation and the many efforts of Christians to resist the logic of reconciliation. At the heart of the Eucharist is the continual reaffirmation and consolidation of personal and collective human identities initially brought about in Baptism. Christian disciples are bound into solidarity with those they have not chosen or whose presence they have not negotiated and indeed would not choose of their own free will. Consequently, the new community, the new world, spoken of in Baptism and the Eucharist is deeply subversive of humanly constructed social order.[10]

The Eucharist does not simply bind individuals to God in a vertical relationship or bind people to each other in another kind of purely social construction. We are bound to one another *en Christo*. And Christ, the head of the body, is to be found persistently on the margins among those who are the least in the kingdom of the world. The margins include those who are other, foreign, strange, dangerous, subversive—even socially, morally, or religiously distasteful in our eyes. Yet the Eucharist insists that humans find solidarity where they least expect it and, indeed, least want to find it. We recall the story of Francis of Assisi and the leper by means of which he passed from a romantic understanding of God's presence in the natural world to embrace the incarnate God in the excluded "other."

The most challenging dimension of the Eucharist is the question of *recognition*. Who do we recognise as our coheirs with Christ, and who are we able to respond to in the real presence of Jesus Christ? The core of the Eucharistic notion of real presence, however one understands this, is *God's* critical recognition of us; God's affirming and life-giving gaze. All are incorporated solely because of God's recognition. The demands on those who practice the Eucharist are consequently more powerful than any notion of solidarity based solely on a social theory, however inclusive or just it seeks to be.[11]

---

10 See Williams, *On Christian Theology*, chapter 14, "Sacraments of the New Society."
11 Williams, *On Christian Theology*, 212–14.

An affirmation of "real presence" also stands in judgment on all our exclusions and negative judgments. Who and what we receive with Jesus is a most challenging question. In receiving Jesus Christ the disciple receives at the same time all that makes up his Body. We find ourselves in communion not merely in some romantic way with the whole court of heaven, a communion of saints that safely visits us from elsewhere and represents merely the past and the future. We also find ourselves, if we dare to name it, in communion with the truly Catholic "mystery of the whole" in present time and space as well. We know from the gospel narratives of the Last Supper that the catholicity of Jesus' act of incorporation included not only disciples like Peter who denied him but Judas who betrayed him. Those we prefer to exclude from communion with us in the public world are already uncomfortable ghosts at our Eucharistic feast.

## Conclusion

The vocation of reconciliation poses the critical question of how much difference we feel able to live with. Being "in communion" with one another is paradoxically both less than and more than complete harmony. It is above all else a risky commitment to one another within a single Body of Christ. Being in communion implies "living in the same house." Being in communion is a commitment to shared conversation—with each other but within a much deeper shared conversation with God. One might say that, like the Christian life more broadly, it is a Trinitarian principle—that who or what we are, we are *only* as we are together.

Reconciliation is only possible if there is a moral willingness to stand back from anger and distaste in order to discern God's will and to embrace God's "catholicity." The problem is that God's will is assumed to be something fully *known* rather than something that we must patiently, prayerfully, and painfully discern. Christian discernment is not a programme or method but an attitude of heart and a delicate process of seeking a necessary spiritual freedom. Such freedom begins by knowing our own continual blindness. To be truly capable of discernment and open to God's will, we leave our preferred judgments and defer to the movements of grace. This demands great Christian maturity.

Spiritual discernment has arisen naturally and most necessarily for such a common life, because it reflects the pressure of a living truth—refusing partiality and bias, pushing beyond individual understanding, opening the discerning community to the creative, self-sharing life from which all truth springs.[12]

Living in a common house is a commitment to conversation as a virtue in itself. Pascal suggested, "A man does not show his greatness by being at one

---

12  See Mark McIntosh, *Discernment and Truth: The Spirituality and Theology of Knowledge* (New York: Crossroad, 2004), 255.

extremity but rather by touching both at once." "Mutuality," the principle of respecting diverse perspectives, involves renunciation—an asceticism, a disciplined "letting go" of any claim to exclusive insight. Most of all, we should cease to pretend to see with the eyes of God. That is idolatry. Without any doubt this form of self-denial in favour of catholicity and reconciliation is not only painful but costly.

# 6

# ESSAYS AND REVIEWS
# 150 YEARS ON[1]

*Mark D. Chapman*

> I often think it's comical
> How nature always does contrive
> That every boy and every gal
> That's born into the world alive
> Is either a little Liberal
> Or else a little Conservative.[2]

There is some truth in W. S. Gilbert's satirical words from *Iolanthe*—people undoubtedly swing towards one party or another, although, of course, in contemporary British politics, it does not always make too much difference. Something similar is often the case in religion—there are some who are inclined towards conservative understandings of doctrine and Scripture. On this model, the Bible is the infallible guide to moral problems, and the church speaks with dogmatic certainty. On the other hand, others in the church are far more likely to side with liberals, and read the Bible in a completely different way—as human reflections on the divine—and to see the church as a frail human institution, capable of making grave mistakes. Such people do not usually feel particularly anxious about changes in theology and church order. As is evident from the recent history of the Anglican Communion, most conservatives will be anxious about issues such as the legitimacy of women bishops, the ordination of practising homosexuals, and the marriage of divorcees; most liberals, however, simply cannot understand why the church has waited for so long to adapt itself to the contemporary world, and see such things as positive developments.

---

1  This essay appeared as an article in the April 2011 issue of *Modern Believing*. Used with permission.
2  From W. S. Gilbert and Arthur Sullivan, *Iolanthe*. This article began life as a lecture given in St. Peter's Church, Brackley, to celebrate the 150th anniversary of the South Northamptonshire Clerical Society in September 2010.

The divisions between conservatives and liberals in the church are obviously not a recent phenomenon—what I will do in this chapter is to outline an earlier controversy which illustrates one such division from the 1860s which shook the church for several years. While it is important to exercise caution when drawing historical parallels, it seems to me that there are some important lessons to be learnt in addressing some of the issues faced by the Church of England and the wider Anglican Communion today. 2010 marks the 150th anniversary of the publication of a book with the unpromising title of *Essays and Reviews*,[3] which became one of the most controversial books in mid-nineteenth-century England. At first sight it is a very strange book: it is a collection of seven completely separate contributions by a number of more or less well-known scholars connected with Oxford, but without any editorial input or much particular direction. All the essays were composed completely independently and there is little coherence in approach or content, which is hardly surprising given that the collected work was a novel genre. Nevertheless, almost immediately after its publication, the book created an enormous stir in the Church of England; in fact it proved more controversial at the time than the publication of Darwin's *Origin of Species* the previous year. The fallout from the publication in some ways resembled the church situation of today—there were threats of division and efforts to work out how structures of authority could be set up to adjudicate in controversies. And yet in the longer term the crisis subsided. Ultimately liberals and conservatives learnt how to live together, perhaps not in a coalition, but at least in a relationship (usually) of mutual understanding and trust.

Discussion of *Essays and Reviews* was not restricted to the universities and learned journals. It also shook the Church of England down into the parishes and deaneries: clergy at the grassroots were frequently agitated, and were prepared to sign petitions. One example comes from the South Northamptonshire Clerical Society, which was established in the same year as the publication of *Essays and Reviews*. The Society, which is still going strong today, was one of many such societies across the country established for groups of local clergy to discuss and debate theological topics and to study the Bible. The early minutes books of the Society show that a number of interesting themes were under discussion, which were no doubt hotly debated issues at the time.[4] The meetings of the first years reflect the mood of mid-Victorian England—some reveal an interest in mission and settlement overseas, including prairie farming and emigration, as well as issues current in the church, such as training for the ministry. But there are hints as well that the clergy were also excited by the issues of biblical interpretation and the limits

---

3   *Essays and Reviews* (London: Parker, 1860). The work rapidly went through a number of editions and modifications. References are to the tenth edition (London: Longmans, 1862). There is a now a critical edition which also makes available a great deal of the critical literature: *Essays and Reviews: The 1860 Text and Its Reading*, ed. Victor Shea and William Whitla (Charlottesville, VA, and London: University Press of Virginia, 2000).

4   I am grateful to the Revd. Peter Woodward for making this information available to me.

of belief raised in *Essays and Reviews*. While in South Northamptonshire much of the Clerical Society's time was spent discussing the Greek text of the New Testament and reading through the books of the Bible, beginning with 1 Timothy, there are nevertheless hints that the clergy were concerned with the wider implications of critical scholarship on their faith. Even at the very first meeting on 14 September 1860 some of the five clergy present were anxious that the ordination oath to "drive away all erroneous and strange doctrines contrary to God's word" was under threat. It is quite feasible that at this meeting the clergy of South Northamptonshire were responding to *Essays and Reviews*, which was felt by many in the church more widely to be watering down the truths of the Christian faith by questioning the inerrancy of Scripture. The contributors appeared to be denying their ordination oaths.

In varying degrees most of the contributions to *Essays and Reviews* presented a version of Christianity which seemed quite at odds with the prevailing theological norms which were held in different ways both among Anglo-Catholics and evangelicals: this comes as no surprise since it represented the first major effort to apply critical scholarship to the Bible in English, and it also reviewed a number of prominent books from Germany,[5] which was regarded by many at the time as a hotbed of radical and dangerous scholarship.[6] Very soon after publication a number of church leaders from both ends of the church began to gather huge petitions to try to have the two beneficed clergy who had contributed (Rowland Williams and H. B. Wilson) removed from their livings. In turn, there was a lengthy court case: the charge brought before the Judicial Committee of the Privy Council was that the clergymen in question had taught doctrines contrary to their ordination vows (even though they were eventually acquitted).

A typical conservative response to *Essays and Reviews* came from Henry Parry Liddon, Edward Pusey's future biographer and first vice-principal of Cuddesdon Theological College. On 31 March 1860, shortly after the book's publication, he wrote to John Keble, expressing his anxiety about the spread of what he called "Rationalism":

> There is a volume of 'Essays and Reviews,' published by J. W. Parker, which has just appeared, and which seems to go further in the race of Rationalism than anything which I have yet seen. Between Jowett's and Wilson's essays, the Gospel history simply evaporates; as Jowett considers the three first Gospels to be merely three forms of one tradition, but 'not three independent witnesses' to our Lord's sayings and acts . . . , and Wilson sees in St. John an element of legendary and ideal embellishment, which contrasts disadvantageously with the predominant moral element of the 'Synoptic' Gospels. Certainly nothing nowadays seems to

---

5   See especially Rowland Williams, "Bunsen's Biblical Researches," in *Essays and Reviews*, 59–111, and Baden Powell, "On the Study of the Evidences of Christianity," 112–72.

6   See Samuel Wilberforce, "Article VIII: Essays and Reviews," *Quarterly Review* 109, no. 217 (January 1861): 248–305, esp. 294–95.

'make a sensation' excepting only the Catholic teaching, as if the principle of rationalism had been generally admitted and it was merely a question of degrees. This book has already sold *largely* in Oxford.[7]

Writing again to Keble a few weeks later from Salisbury, he noted that he had brought the book to Bishop Walter Kerr Hamilton's notice (and in whose diocese Rowland Williams held the living of Broade Chalke): "What he will do, I don't know. He insists much upon the necessity of large consideration for others, as a condition of holding things at all together. Of course, it becomes a question of limits."[8] And this, it seems to me, is what is most important if we are to learn any lessons for today: the "question of limits" which Liddon raises remains a perennial problem for the church—indeed the limits of diversity remain as hotly contested in our own day as they were in the 1860s. The questions are still these: How can diversity be held together? How can conservatives and liberals learn to live together in "coalition" or at least with "the necessity of a large consideration for others"?

*Essays and Reviews* created a stir principally because it raised questions about the limits to the diversity of belief, especially among the clergy. In England the questions that the book raised, if not entirely unprecedented, were relatively novel.[9] While much of what the book said had been said earlier (and usually better) in Germany, some of the essays, especially Benjamin Jowett's on "The Interpretation of Scripture," which was the longest and probably the most influential in the volume,[10] were the first full-scale popular discussions of a critical way of reading the Bible. Jowett, who at the time was Regius Professor of Greek at Oxford, and shortly afterwards became Master of Balliol, was one of the leading scholars of his day, which meant that his views carried weight. While he recognised in his essay that the interpretation of Scripture required "'a vision and faculty divine,'" he nevertheless held that "in the externals of interpretation, that is to say, the meaning of words, the connexion of sentences, the settlement of the text, the evidence of facts, the same rules apply to the Old and New Testaments as to other books."[11] That was obviously a highly contested statement in 1860. Jowett was secure in his faith that God's truth was to be discovered both within and outside the Christian tradition. "The education of the human mind," he wrote, "may be traced as clearly from the book of Genesis to the Epistles of St Paul, as from Homer to Plato and Aristotle."[12]

It was Jowett's dictum which called on the reader to *"interpret the*

---

7  John Octavius Johnston, *Life and Letters of Henry Parry Liddon* (London: Longmans, 1904), 63–64.

8  *Ibid.*, 64.

9  See, for instance, John Rogerson, *Old Testament Criticism in the Nineteenth Century: England and Germany* (London: SPCK, 1984), esp. 180–220.

10  Benjamin Jowett, 'The Interpretation of Scripture', in *Essays and Reviews*, 399–527.

11  *Ibid.*, 407–8.

12  *Ibid*, 487. I have discussed liberalism and the philosophy of education, particularly in relation to Frederick Temple's essay, "The Education of the World" (pp. 1–58), in "The Authority of Reason? The Importance of Being Liberal," in *The Hope of Things to Come*, ed. Mark D. Chapman (London: Mowbray, 2010), 45–68.

*Scripture like any other book*"[13] that so provoked more conservative readers of Scripture, who tended to approach Scripture with such a degree of reverence and awe that they found it difficult to ask scholarly questions even about genre and textual transmission, which were Jowett's main concerns. Jowett's many opponents included Samuel Wilberforce, bishop of Oxford, who immediately after its publication sought to condemn the book and its authors by means of the recently revived Convocation. On Wilberforce's view, to be sceptical in religion or to adopt a critical stance was an assault against the truths disclosed once and for all through revelation. Shortly after publication Wilberforce wrote a lengthy and often vitriolic article for the *Quarterly Review* where he criticised the essays in turn. Although he differentiated between the essays, he nevertheless felt that all the authors had to be grouped together since it was the book as a whole that provoked controversy, even if some of the essays were less problematic for conservative readers. Wilberforce was particularly upset that Frederick Temple, headmaster of Rugby and one of the leading educationalists of the day, should have consented to having his essay included alongside what he called the "scarcely-veiled Atheism of Mr. Baden Powell" and the "open scepticism and laxity of Mr. Wilson."[14] Wilberforce simply could not understand how the writers could "with moral honesty maintain their posts as clergymen in the Established Church."[15] For Wilberforce, the sort of critical theology the authors had displayed amounted to the thin end of the wedge. Returning to issues that had been much debated the previous century, he argued that if Christ's miracles were denied then the divinity of Christ was put into question. Thus Wilberforce could write: "If he wrought the works, the whole rationalistic scheme crumbles into dust; if He wrought not the works, claiming as he claimed to work them as the very proofs of his mission, He was, in truth, the deceiver that the chief priests declared him to be."[16] For Wilberforce a great deal was at stake.

Wilberforce consequently orchestrated a discussion among all the bishops of the Church of England (and Wales) early in 1861, and a number, including R. D. Hampden of Hereford (himself under suspicion by Newman and Pusey as a liberal earlier in his career), thought that prosecution was necessary. *Essays and Reviews*, Hampden held, had provoked such a crisis in the church that it was nothing less than a question of "Christianity or no Christianity."[17] In the end all twenty-six bishops signed the archbishop of Canterbury's letter of 12 February which stated that "we cannot understand how these opinions can be held consistently with an honest subscription to the formularies of our Church, with many of the fundamental doctrines of which they appear

---

13 Jowett, "The Interpretation of Scripture," in *Essays and Reviews*, 458 (Jowett's italics).
14 Samuel Wilberforce, "Article VIII: Essays and Reviews," *Quarterly Review* 109, no. 217 (January 1861): 248–305, esp. 251.
15 *Ibid.*, 302.
16 *Ibid.*, 283.
17 Cited in Reginald G. Wilberforce, *Life of the Right Reverend Samuel Wilberforce, D.D.* (London: John Murray, 1882), 3:3.

to us essentially at variance."[18] The bishops were very clear about the limits of belief among the clergy and they appeared to be exercising decisive leadership. Wilberforce, together with many of his fellow bishops, continued to campaign vigorously against the book, which, as he put it in his 1863 charge to his clergy, reflected the rationalist tendency or "an endeavour to get rid of all belief in the personal acting amidst us of any supernatural power, whether in the realms of matter or spirit."[19]

Huge petitions were gathered from evangelicals and Anglo-Catholics in a relatively rare moment of common endeavour. In the end, the court case dragged on for a number of years, before finally finishing indecisively in 1864. The authors were not silenced permanently and the book continued to be read in large numbers.[20] Pusey, never prone to understatement, thought that the crisis provoked by *Essays and Reviews* and the failure of the courts to censure the writers was "a struggle for the life and death of the Church of England."[21] "Without some combined effort to repudiate the Judgment," he wrote to Wilberforce, "the Church of England will be destroyed or will become the destroyer of souls."[22] So much for the limits of diversity, at least according to the bishops and some of the leading churchmen of the time. But within thirty years one of the essayists (Frederick Temple) had become archbishop of Canterbury: thought had moved on and what was acceptable had changed. Firm and decisive leadership by bishops had proved both ineffectual and ultimately pointless.

## Conclusion

The controversies following from the publication of *Essays and Reviews* in 1860 provide a good illustration of the sorts of issues which have divided and continue to divide clergy and theologians. The questions that emerge reflect different approaches to the interpretation of Scripture, and different understandings of truth, and of how that truth is to be tested. But they also reveal something of the complexities involved in leadership in the church. Many clamoured for decisive and quick action, which would silence those who seemed to be pushing things too far in what seemed a dangerous direction. And these questions, it seems to me, are as present in the Anglican Communion today as they were in the 1860s. Indeed, although it would be wrong to push things too far, there are some parallels between *Essays and*

---

18  *Ibid.*, 3:5. See also William Benham, *Life of Archibald Campbell Tait* (London: Macmillan, 1891), 1:282–83.

19  Samuel Wilberforce, *A Charge Delivered to the Diocese of Oxford, at His Sixth Visitation, November, 1863* (Oxford: Parker, 1863), 45.

20  On the controversies surrounding *Essays and Reviews*, see Ieuan Ellis, *Seven against Christ: A Study of Essays and Reviews* (Leiden: Brill, 1980); and Josef L. Altholz, *Anatomy of a Controversy: The Debate over Essays and Reviews* (Aldershot: Scholar Press, 1994). See also Basil Willey, *More Nineteenth Century Studies: A Group of Honest Doubters* (Cambridge: Cambridge University Press, 1956), ch. 4; and A. O. J. Cockshut, *Anglican Attitudes* (London: Collins, 1959), ch. 4.

21  Pusey to Stanley, 23 February 1864, in H. P. Liddon, *The Life of E. B. Pusey* (London: Longmans, 1897), 4:63.

22  Pusey to Wilberforce, 13 February 1864, in *ibid.*, 52.

*Reviews* and the contemporary situation in the Anglican Communion. Let me take just one example. As is well known, the final amended text of Resolution 1.10 from the 1998 Lambeth Conference called on the Lambeth Conference to "listen to the experience of homosexual people" but at the same time it adopted the following clause:

> *while rejecting homosexual practice as incompatible with Scripture,* [the Conference] calls on all our people to minister pastorally and sensitively to all irrespective of sexual orientation and to condemn *irrational fear of homosexuals*, violence within marriage and any trivialisation and commercialisation of sex.[23]

If Scripture is regarded as "containing all things necessary to salvation" (Article VII) and as the basis for moral norms—which is one of the most undisputed principles of Anglican method and which had been reaffirmed at the same Conference—and if the bishops were seen as its authoritative interpreters, then the short amended subclause which regards "homosexual practice as incompatible with Scripture" rules out the legitimacy of all forms of homosexual practice. While earlier Lambeth Conferences had issued resolutions, advice, and commitments, this particular clause was more far-reaching: the overwhelming majority of the bishops in the Anglican Communion had ruled that something was incompatible with Scripture. This had been done only twice before, once on a sexual matter, with Resolution 19 from 1930 noting that "illicit and irregular unions are wrong and contrary to the revealed will of God," and once on the illegitimacy of racism and tribalism (1978, Resolution 3). Possibly because of this Scriptural underpinning, Resolution 1.10 was treated very differently from Lambeth Resolutions of the past. In many quarters it has come to be regarded as a magisterial teaching of the Anglican Communion and has been elevated into something like a test of soundness or orthodoxy. Homosexuality was and always would be contrary to Scripture. Diversity of interpretation on this issue, it seems, was rejected, which has led to the slow process which has resulted in a proposed Anglican Covenant. The bishops had made a decisive judgment with far-reaching implications.

And yet, as Lambeth 2008 demonstrated, it was still possible to hold contrary opinions, and to be respected and listened to by others: a widely accepted moral norm which had been elevated by many to the status of a dogma, and which was supported by a large majority of bishops, could nevertheless be questioned through a process of engagement and deep listening. And it was perhaps this attitude of tolerance which demonstrates a possible solution to the problems facing the Anglican Communion. For the most part, after all, people have little to fear from those at the extremes, except perhaps from being forced to think for themselves (as eventually happened with many

---

23 At http://www.anglicancommunion.org/windsor2004/appendix/p3.6.cfm (accessed 2 September 2010). Italics indicate the amendments that were inserted.

opponents after 1860 as they came to accept the legitimacy of the sorts of methods adopted in *Essays and Reviews*). Instead, listening to and learning from those of very different views, provided there are efforts to understand where they are coming from, can serve instead to help others understand their own faith far more deeply (as the archbishop of Canterbury hinted in his presidential addresses in 2008).[24]

Through the last century and a half, clergy and laity in the Church of England and across the wider Anglican Communion have frequently campaigned for and against many causes which seemed to threaten the unity of the church. Sometimes it looked as if opinion was firmly set against those of a more liberal disposition. Although occasionally—even if not very often—there have been splits, for the most part the church has weathered the storms and has survived pretty much unscathed. And quite often it has even changed its mind (as the Anglican Communion did over contraception in the first half of the last century and as happened relatively quickly after *Essays and Reviews*) even when opinions seemed quite entrenched. Despite seemingly intractable positions, most people most of the time have been prepared to listen to those with very different opinions and not to break communion (even when they have sometimes wanted to). Decisive actions by bishops tend not to be very effective at solving conflicts in the church, and neither do petitions and legal cases. Listening and learning to live in an uneasy coalition might be a better way even if it lacks clarity and tidiness. Contemporary British politics might thus have something to teach the Anglican Communion.

---

24 See my introduction in Mark Chapman, Martyn Percy, Ian Markham, and Barney Hawkins, eds., *Christ and Culture: Communion after Lambeth*, Canterbury Studies in Anglicanism (Norwich: Canterbury Press, 2010), 1–27.

# 7

## *KOINONIA* AS THE FIRST GIFT OF THE SPIRIT

### Communication, Consensus, Communion

*Robert D. Hughes III*

### Church of the Holy Sepulcher

Earlier this month Barbara and I were privileged to make our first pilgrimage to Jerusalem. One of the highlights of any such visit is, of course, the great basilica of the Holy Sepulcher. We were deeply moved by the opportunity to pray at what may well have been Calvary, inside what may well have been the empty tomb, and, unexpectedly, at the "Stone of the Anointing" in between. It is an experience that has stuck with me as I think and pray in the aftermath. But—and those of you who have been there know what is coming— there is another side to the experience. One gets to the church by entering a clearly Israeli City (with a contested shared claim by Palestine over the Eastern sector), wending a way through what is left of the Christian quarter, to reach the basilica located in the Arab/Muslim quarter. One of the first things the guide points out is a ladder that has been on the façade for centuries, because nothing can be changed without the consent of all the groups that share jurisdiction in the church, and they have been unable to agree on removing the ladder. Then there are the Ethiopians on the roof, and the Armenian shrine tacked onto the back of the sepulcher itself. So what one finds at the Christian heart of a city riven by the sibling quarrels of the Family of Abraham is a church contested for centuries by competing Christian jurisdictions, all of ancient lineage. Many of the groups are party to quite successful ecumenical discussions in the modern era, but the progress is not apparent in the icon of Christian *koinonia* presented by its most sacred edifice. The church falls into ever-deeper disrepair because agreement cannot be found about what to do. At the same time, some degree of family relationship is maintained.

## *Koinonia* Has Always Been a Mess

The Church of the Holy Sepulcher is certainly a profound icon of the paschal mystery, as was intended. But it is also, not intended, an icon of a brutal fact: the common life of the people of God, our communion and fellowship with one another in Christ by the power of the Holy Spirit, is and always has been a mess. As we consider the nature and limits of *koinonia* in the midst of the current crisis in Anglicanism, honesty requires us to start with that admission. There is no golden age to which we can look back for a definitive shape of untroubled *koinonia*. Moses is always having trouble with God's people and bemoaning the task of herding them. The great prophets are always pointing out the rot at the core of the *koinonia* of Israel and Judah and predicting the dire consequences that will result. Just about the time Paul patches it up with Peter and James, along comes Apollos. And on it goes. Even the great Ecumenical Councils, to which I strive to be loyal as an Anglican and a theologian, continue to be marked by the substantial bodies of Christians who did not accept them, groups that Philip Jenkins has made visible to us once again.[1]

The Anglican Communion was born as the consequence of a violent revolution that left the American church out of communion with Canterbury; the restoration of communion required the larger party to stretch the boundaries of *koinonia* by acknowledging that it need not be constructed around the British monarchy. So as we consider the current state of affairs in the Anglican Communion, we shall do best by admitting the reality of the facts on the ground: this is actually the normal state of affairs.

## *Koinonia* as Gift

However, it is also true that *koinonia* is the first gift of the Holy Spirit to the people of God, a self-donation by which that common life becomes the fellowship of the Body of Christ. The last two decades have seen the rise of "Spirit-Christology," exploring the fullness of the intertwined missions of Word and Spirit in the Christological mysteries. This emphasis is well expressed by the simplicity of Killian McDonnell's statement that "The Holy Spirit is the mediation of that of which Christ is the mediator."[2] In concert with this Spirit-Christology there has emerged a "Spirit Ecclesiology," emphasizing the people of God as the fellowship of the Spirit and hence as the Body of Christ. Following St. Paul, to be in the Spirit is thus to be also in Christ, as a mystical reality, not merely a metaphor. An excellent representative of this

---

1  Philip Jenkins, *The Lost History of Christianity: The Thousand-Year Golden Age of the Church in the Middle East, Africa, and Asia—and How It Died* (New York: HarperOne, 2008); see also *Jesus Wars* (New York: HarperOne, 2010).

2  Kilian McDonnell, *The Other Hand of God: The Holy Spirit as the Universal Touch and Goal* (Collegeville, MN: Liturgical Press, 2003), 103–7, 112–14. For an excellent treatment of the literature and theological issues of Spirit-Christology, see Ralph Del Colle, *Christ and the Spirit: Spirit-Christology in Trinitarian Perspective* (New York and Oxford: Oxford University Press, 1994).

Spirit-ecclesiology is Bradford Hinze at Fordham.[3] In a recent conversation he noted that if we place too much emphasis on the Spirit as the *koinonia* of the church, it can end up supporting the hierarchical institutional rigidity that is a constant temptation on one side. The balance, he stated at a recent event, is to remember that the Spirit is also the Spirit of Prophecy. The same Spirit who binds us together is also the one who defends the poor and excluded and blows where she will. Another attendee at the same event, the Rev. Dr. Dan Hall, an Episcopalian, reminded us that the danger on the other side is that everyone wishing to act out ego needs can claim the spirit of prophecy. But the fundamental point remains: *koinonia* is at the Spirit's disposal, not ours, because *koinonia* is the Spirit as self-donation, and the same Spirit is also the Spirit of prophecy, blowing where she will.

So we have these two facts on the ground: *koinonia* is the Spirit's own self-gift, and the reality is that the *koinonia* of the people of God is typically a conflicted mess.

## The Holy Spirit and the Boundaries of *Koinonia*

The Spirit resists most efforts to tidy up the *koinonia*, and when the Spirit does intervene, it is (almost?) always on the side of expanding boundaries, not contracting them. As Gene Rogers points out, the Spirit is always resting on the unsavable other and inviting the church to include them.[4] *Semper Reformanda* equals *semper expandanda* until at the *parousia* the Beloved Community embraces the whole human race. An exception is Simon Magus (Acts 8). Some things are clearly beyond the Spirit's *koinonia*, not because the Spirit has laid aside the mode of prophecy, but because that mode itself critiques that which excludes itself from *koinonia*. The desire to control the power of the Spirit as a kind of magic is clearly one such exclusion. The council at Jerusalem listed others, including the notorious *"porneia,"* which some critics limit to marriage of prohibited degree, while others interpret to mean any sexual activity outside heterosexual monogamy. I would like to think that the modern sense is actually correct: *porneia* is any activity with sexual overtones that treats the other as merely an object for my own satisfaction and not as a full person who as such holds the key to my own being. But let's acknowledge the present reality—here is actually the contested locus of our current debate, and the most honest answer is that we just don't know by definition whether some homosexual relationships are "nonpornographic" in the sense that some heterosexual relations may be. The testimony of faithful Christians who are in faithful same-sex relationships is simply "yes," and I confess I am among those who are persuaded by them to discern the Spirit as sacramentally active

---

3   Bradford E. Hinze, "Releasing the Power of the Spirit in a Trinitarian Ecclesiology," in *Advents of the Spirit*, ed. Bradford E. Hinze and D. Lyle Dabney (Milwaukee: Marquette University Press, 2001), 347–81. The event referred to subsequently was the Holy Spirit Colloquium at Duquesne University, September 17, 2010.

4   Eugene F. Rogers, Jr., *After the Spirit: A Constructive Pneumatology from Resources Outside the Modern West* (Grand Rapids: Wm. B. Eerdmans Publishing Co., 2005), 85–97.

in their common life as "the church in miniature" in the same sense as in solemnized heterosexual marriages. But this ground is severely contested. So I would state the situation thusly: in most cases the Spirit seems to be trying to expand the *koinonia* of the church to a degree that is always shocking to those already within the fellowship. The Spirit seems willing to put up with, even to cause, a certain amount of messiness in the *koinonia* for the sake of this expansion. Nevertheless, there are limits, though these are to be discerned by the fellowship, not legislated to our taste. The boundaries are set by the Spirit, not by us; we can only seek to discern them. As a general rule our discernment will turn out to have been too narrow and the Spirit is quite likely to violate boundaries we have set for the sake of inviting in the prostitutes, tax collectors, and other sinners. On the matter in current dispute, the biblical evidence is ambivalent.

## The Spirit and the Sectarian Principle

At the same time, there is something seriously wrong with the sectarian principle, which is often confused with the Protestant principle. *Semper Reformanda* should not mean that at the drop of a hat I will break communion with you and start my own church. Hinze seems to me to get it exactly right in his essay on Spirit-Ecclesiology in the volume *Advents of the Spirit*. I quote two entire paragraphs simply because I find them so spot on:

> The Spirit's summons to a more genuine catholicity is a hard calling because it pulls and pushes the church to grow, to a deeper conversion, and when needed to institutional change at the local and universal level. Such change is not in the interest of faddish innovation or at the expense of the gospel of Christ, the apostolic heritage and offices, but rather is pursued in fidelity to the gifts of God. The Spirit's call to catholicity symbolized at Pentecost and epitomized by the initial Hellenistic mission is but the further realization and ongoing evolution of the catholicity of Jesus' mission in Galilee to those at the margins, those religiously and socially disconnected, those who have yearned to be released from the destructive powers at work in the world and in their own personal lives by the power of God's reign.
>
> In some cases the Spirit's appeal for greater catholicity can appear to risk tearing the church apart through disagreement and disunity: the debates about liberation, inculturation, and relativism offer ample evidence. But perhaps this agitation is in the interest of purgation, sanctification, and the holiness of the church. As contentious as these debates can sometimes be, one thing we know for certain: factionalism cannot be the ultimate outcome, for the Spirit that beckons to catholicity also lures to communion, *koinonia*, the friendship of the Holy Spirit.[5]

---

5   Hinze, "Releasing the Power of the Spirit in a Trinitarian Ecclesiology," in *Advents of the Spirit*, 370.

What can we conclude from these observations so far? It seems to me the Spirit is willing to put up with the mess in *koinonia* in order to keep the boundaries fluid and ever more inclusive. Joseph Dinoia has said that the major remaining question for Christian theology of interfaith dialogue concerns the place in divine providence for the diversity of human religious expression.[6] I think we face a similar question here: what is the place in divine providence for the messiness of the *koinonia* of the church? I would like to suggest one possible clue.

## Understanding the Mess

According to Jesuit theologian Luis Bermejo, in his highly nuanced discussion of the Spirit and the *sensus fidelium*, the mess in the *koinonia* has a structure, a four-fold cycle of communication, conflict, consensus, communion, that derives from the tension between the Spirit as the source of authority and the Spirit as a Spirit of freedom.[7] He sees this process as not only unavoidable, but as essential, if the process of discerning the *sensus fidelium* is to be genuine and reliable. "Communication, conflict, consensus, communion: these four steps in various degrees of intensity are a must if the much vaunted faith-sense is to achieve its purpose of preserving and deepening the Christian faith." Notice the purpose, for here, I think, we find a possible answer for why the Spirit seems to prefer the messiness of actual *koinonia*: it is out of such a mess, and not out of an imposed order, that the Christian faith is deepened by new theological insight.

We do not have the option of deciding for ourselves what sort of era we shall inhabit in that cycle. The issue for us today is thus: how do we live faithfully in a period of conflict? Our own times have some particular difficulties that must be faced. Looking at the four-fold cycle as a whole will help us accept our current place and also better manage our own peculiar difficulties.

**Communication.** Bermejo defines this as follows: "The faithful should be enlightened by their pastors, for the opinion of an unenlightened crowd is often worthless. . . ." Here, I think we should note two things: First, we are emerging from an era in which the gospel and the Catholic faith have been ill-taught to the people. Programs like EFM (Education for Ministry) have made a significant dent, but we have a long way to go. A wonderful semester at one of the leading theological colleges in Africa has only reinforced for me the belief that theological education for clergy and laity around the world is a vital necessity, and that the conditions for a genuine and reliable *sensus fidelium* do not currently exist on the ground. TEAC (Theological Education for

6   J. A. Dinoia, O. P., *The Diversity of Religions: A Christian Perspective* (Washington DC: Catholic University of America Press, 1992), 91.

7   Luis Bermejo, S. J, *The Spirit of Life: The Holy Spirit in the Life of the Christian* (Anand, Gujarat, India: Gujarat Sahitya Prakash, 1987; printed and distributed in the U.S. by Loyola University Press), 360 (see also 300–330). In fn. 19, p. 360, he cites L. Sartori, "What Is the Criterion for the 'Sensus Fidelium'?" *Concilium* (Oct. 1980): 56–60.

the Anglican Communion) should receive full support, and, I believe, if it is to be an instrument for forming the *sensus fidelium*, it should become a structure of the Anglican Consultative Council, not just the Primates, and place more emphasis on lay education, without neglecting training for ordinands.

Second, communication is now much more rapid than ever before. An immediate benefit is that there are technological resources available for our task of theological education that could greatly enhance its reach and power, and we have only begun to explore those possibilities. But communication is also now so rapid that what I say here may well be critiqued in, say, Lagos, even before you have finished reading this book. There is little time to read, mark, learn, and inwardly digest. Furthermore, the effort to make one's own voice heard above the digital din usually involves ramping up the volume and the rhetoric. The rhetoric of blogging is not conducive to actually working through theological issues. One way to be faithful in a time such as ours would be to commit to respectful communication on both sides, using a rhetoric designed to work through theological issues, not perpetuate them.

**Conflict.** Clearly we live in this part of the cycle, with much of the struggle being about human sexuality, but as a stalking horse for several very old issues in theological argument:

One is an argument over what it means to interpret Scripture faithfully. Within Anglicanism we currently run the gamut from those who insist on a traditional evangelical reading of everything based on "the plain sense of the text" to Jack Spong and Marcus Borg. I think we search for some consensus on a *range* of interpretation that is both critical and faithful, and I believe that the great biblical scholars of the Westcott era can point the way for us. The current project on the use of Scripture in the Anglican Communion seems spot on to me as a fruitful opportunity for mutual enlightenment.

A second issue is the reemergence in Christian ethics of the tension between law-based versus character/virtue-based ethics in Christian life. This came out in discussions at the meeting of the Episcopal Church Foundation Fellows in Philadelphia. In response to an argument I was making from Anglican casuistry, my good friend Paul Zahl responded with an evangelical argument that casuistry is always a compromise with the gold standard in ethics. This is a tension within Anglican ethics between puritan and catholic that has been with us from the start, and I believe it deeply shapes much of the current conflicts. I wish we could find a forum and get it out on the table, and I confess my own prejudice that we have the resources for a *modus vivendi* here in the wisdom of the Caroline Divines and their unique approach to casuistry.

A third issue is far too large to deal with today: who has the responsibility for discerning that an argument, though still echoing, has nevertheless been resolved, so that a consensus can be discerned? In the Roman Catholic context this is an ongoing debate about the papacy and its relationship to the college of bishops. Within Anglicanism, it is the sometimes inelegant jockeying for place among the so-called instruments of communion, as we continue to live with the typical muddle of a British-style constitution based on common law with many seeming to long for a more clearly stated continental-style order based on Roman law. Much too big to deal with today, but a serious theological question for us is this: is the commitment of Anglicanism to a common law pastoral governance in contrast to a Roman law juridical governance not one of the gifts we bring to the ecumenical table? If it is, then we would be ill advised to jump ship precisely at this juncture, just because the going has gotten rough.

Fourth is a further issue about the rhetoric with which we address one another. Here I rely on the work of a former student of mine, Gayle Browne, and a former teacher, Herb Richardson, who has said that he thinks the demon of our age is ideological conflict.[8] Indeed, the rhetoric of ideological conflict treats the opponent as incapable of truth and salvation, and is useful for whipping up enthusiasm in people who already agree with you and getting them to give and volunteer, but is useless for persuading people who disagree with you. Its vested interest is in perpetuating conflict, not resolving it, so it is useless for resolving conflicts. All of our public life is infected with this rhetoric, as the recent American campaigns for elections have made clear. The reason is simple: follow the money. In the current mess, the role of the Institute on Religion and Democracy and its schemes on the so-called traditionalist side have yet to be fully told, and I don't doubt there are corporate sponsors for the progressive side as well. This ideological rhetoric has become so ingrained in many that any shift to a rhetoric of *koinonia* and conflict resolution is considered unfaithful. And yet, I suggest the opposite: faithfulness in a time of conflict means sacrificing short-term self-interest by leaving aside the rhetoric of ideological conflict and adopting rhetoric and strategies of conflict resolution. Certainly the Indaba process at Lambeth intended that, and I would cite Rowan Williams' own belief that one major form of unfaithfulness is seeking to bring premature closure to a theological argument. Ideological rhetoric does that by definition, and we must forswear it.

If I may be permitted an aside. I certainly understand how difficult life is at the moment for those administering the "instruments of communion." I believe they felt compelled to exercise some discipline on the American church after the consecration of Mary Glasspool, and I am delighted that some even-handedness has finally been shown in also disciplining the Southern Cone for incursions, though the same questions need to be raised for several African provinces as well. I believe those seeking a solution thought that removing people from the ecumenical and faith and order discussions was the lightest slap on the wrist they could come up with. But the danger that is now faced is this: if the progressive voice is progressively removed from the table, then

---

8 Gayle Hansen Browne, "Feminist Rhetoric and Christological Discourse: Conflict or Conversion," MA thesis, Sewanee: University of the South, 1993; Herbert W. Richardson, *Toward an American Theology* (New York: Harper & Row, 1967).

agreements reached will be unacceptable to a large part of the communion, the risk of a schism on the left becomes real, and I am not speaking of just the North American churches. Enough on that for the present.

**Consensus.** This is the trickiest bit, as it requires someone or a group of someones to discern a common mind in the church. It is certainly not enough merely to take a poll or a vote. Not even unanimity is good enough, as "You can fool all of the people some of the time." Part of the discernment must be about the maturity of the argument and the level of enlightened participation in it, as well as a sense of "counting the house." Bermejo calls this *sensus*

> a kind of spiritual instinct by which the faithful sense and detect what is genuinely Christian, what is in keeping with the Gospel, what clicks or clashes with the message of Christ. . . . It is a kind of intuitive grasp of what is consonant with the Christian truth, a sort of charism of discernment by means of which the simple, often unlettered faithful can tell truth from error. It is not only through hierarchical structures, but also through this intuitive, instinctual faith that the Holy Spirit maintains the Church in the truth.[9]

Nicely said, but the problems abound. As we have already noted, the issue of who gets to be part of discerning this charism of consensus is deeply contested within Anglicanism at the moment. We also have to ask about what happens when the hierarchy ignore a growing consensus they don't like, such as birth control, or the desire to open the priesthood to married men and women both married and single. These are no longer issues for much of the Anglican world, but the results in the Roman Catholic world are telling: mostly the people just ignore what they can't swallow. Nevertheless, clarity does somehow seem to emerge out of the muddle, and, when it is announced, the vast majority of Christians will be able to agree with it, even if not at the level of dogma. Hinze describes it as follows:

> In humble and mutual receptivity to the work of the Spirit, the entire church is called to be a learning church and a teaching church, where the *sensus fidei* yields a *sensus fidelium*, which provides the conditions of the possibility of a *consensus fidelium* that emerges from the communication action of the traditioning process.[10]

**Communion.** The final desired outcome, at least as we long for it, may be only an eschatological reality. But part of the discernment of a true *sensus fidelium* is that it will edify the church, that is, contribute to its peace and unity in the Spirit and hence in Christ. In times such as ours, we can only long for such unity, pray for it, work for it, forswear methods of argument that impede it, etc. What we cannot do is force it in any way or it shall surely be stillborn. It seems to me that the major commitment needs to be staying

---

9 Bermejo, *The Spirit of Life*, 360.
10 Hinze, "Releasing the Power of the Spirit in a Trinitarian Ecclesiology," in *Advents of the Spirit*, 370.

at the same table with those with whom I most disagree, as long as humanly possible, adopting whenever I can an irenic rhetoric of reconciliation, and working to help make sure that the least-heard voices get heard, all the while praying for the resolution we cannot now even imagine.

One perhaps overly bold conclusion: if any of this is even close to true, then the invocation of the sectarian principle as if it were the Protestant principle, the insistence on bailing out of the messy argument or of insisting that some legitimate voices be excluded from it, could well be the sin against the Holy Spirit. I hope all our leaders will exercise appropriate caution as we seek to navigate an era of conflict so that it may be a gift to us and not a curse. In that light, I must appeal to the archbishop and the secretary general of the Communion to reconsider the decision to exclude from the conversation voices that must be heard if we are to be faithful to the process to which the Spirit appears to be committed as the means for deepening Christian faith and apprehension of truth.

# 8

# THE SHAPE OF THINGS TO COME?

## Two Church of England Parishes in a Time of Transition[1]

*Simon J. Taylor*

Let me begin with a story. At 7 a.m. on Easter morning a group of about eighty people gathered outside a former Congregationalist chapel now used as an Anglican parish church.[2] They came from three groups: the congregation of Cotham Parish Church, where they were all gathered; the congregation of St. Paul's, Clifton, the neighbouring parish that has been together in a united benefice[3] with Cotham Parish Church since 1999; and members of Resonance, an alternative worship community[4] which has strong links to the vicar of the benefice and which has used Cotham Parish Church as a base since his appointment there. So this is the story—three communities coming together to worship.

But there is another way to tell the story. The service began with quite traditional catholic ritual—the lighting of the Paschal candle from a new flame, its procession into church and the singing of the Exsultet. But then, while passages from the Old Testament were read, the congregation was invited to explore some installations relating to them. The story of creation was explored by making figures out of clay; reflecting on the delights and frustrations of being created; and magnetic poetry. Calvin and Hobbes cartoons lent it a humorous flavour. In the installation reflecting on the exodus, one was greeted by Charlton Heston's Moses parting the Red Sea on a video loop.

---

1  Previously published in Ian S. Markham and Martyn Percy, eds., *Why Liberal Churches Are Growing* (Edinburgh: T & T Clark, 2006). Used with permission.

2  At the formation of the United Reformed Church in 1972, the Congregationalist congregation moved into another church building in the area. Two Anglican parishes were being merged and rather than close one church building, both were merged into the former chapel. It was dedicated for Anglican worship in 1975.

3  Technically, the two benefices of the parishes of Cotham and St Paul's, Clifton are held in plurality by the incumbent of both. See Mark Hill, *Ecclesiastical Law*, 2nd ed. (Oxford: Oxford University Press, 2001), 110.

4  On alternative worship, see Paul Roberts, *Alternative Worship in the Church of England*, Grove Worship 155 (Cambridge: Grove, 1999).

Two shower curtains, covered in advertisements and symbols of addictions and imprisonments led to an icon, where candles could be lit and liberations prayed for. In all there were four stations. After some time to explore these, the congregation was called back together by the singing of "Alleluia" for the gospel reading. Then they entered the sanctuary, which had been screened off from the body of the church. Inside was a paddling pool full of water, draped in white cloth with lilies around it. Here baptismal vows were renewed, then people splashed themselves with the water, took a piece of white cloth, and were anointed with oil. Finally, the Eucharist was celebrated, using an authorised Anglican liturgy with ambient music playing in the background and projections of the cosmos on screens overhead. This is story two: an imaginative attempt to marry two very different styles of worship, the gifts of each being offered to enrich the other.

But, you will forgive me, I am a curate and for me the story begins the day before. It takes a great deal of preparation for such an event, and most of Holy Saturday was spent moving furniture, setting up installations, and the like. It also saw a dreadful row between one man setting up part of the service and the lady who arranged the flowers. This led, ultimately, to her leaving the church, at least for now. Story three, therefore, is "how we lost our flower arranger."

There are other ways of telling the story of our Easter vigil, most of which are for others to tell. None of these stories begin or end with the Easter vigil, each are part of a longer history which began before the vigil and continue in the life of the churches today. But the vigil provides a focus for these stories in which they can be identified. I want to suggest that the three stories reflect three different pressures that are felt by these two parishes at the present time. These pressures come from the church, wider society, and also from within the parishes themselves.

## Pressure from the Church

The reason why the Easter vigil service marks the coming together of three communities, two of them parish churches, is that since 1999 the two parishes concerned have been a united benefice. This was a decision made by the Diocese of Bristol at the time of the appointment of the current vicar of the parishes. The effect of this has been that each parish runs separately, whilst sharing ministerial resources in the form of a vicar and, latterly, a curate.[5] From the vigil, the vicar went on to preside at an all-age Eucharist at Cotham, and the curate to do the same at St. Paul's. Ministerial time is not allocated in a fixed way between the parishes, as it might be in the case of a parish job being shared with a diocesan job. Instead a more flexible approach is taken.

Nevertheless, the sharing of resources and the legal status of the parishes

---

5   All licensed ministers, lay and ordained, are licensed to the benefice rather than to either of the individual parishes. Other than the vicar and curate, most minister almost exclusively in one or the other parish.

as a joint benefice sometimes require decisions to be made as a benefice. This creates problems in that very few people see the operation of the benefice *as a benefice* (rather than as a parish within the benefice). Three or four benefice Eucharists a year is the extent of the impact most feel, but even these must be agreed as deviations from the normal pattern of services. The weekly staff meeting is the only decision-making forum that has a benefice wide view, and it has no status to make some of the necessary decisions.[6] Earlier this year, each parish within the deanery was asked to provide an outline of themselves as part of the consideration of future provision of ministry. The clergy of the benefice felt strongly that the two parishes could only do this adequately as a benefice. This required both Parochial Church Councils (PCCs) to assent to a document drafted by the clergy, a rushed process, with complex negotiations required, which did not happen without some resentment.

Recently, the PCCs of both parishes met together for a study day. At the end of the day there was an exercise asking people to say in single words and short phrases how they saw the benefice. Most of the responses described features that the two parishes had in common ("liberal"; "intellectual"; "predominantly old-ish"). Some looked at what might be the case ("waiting to fly"; "open sky"; potential-filled"), and others reflected the experience of being in the benefice. In this latter category, some responses reflected the separateness of the churches and the sharing of ministers: "two churches"; "two parishes"; "vicar-share"; and "Paul [the vicar]." Others spoke of the experience as "theoretical"; "unreal"; "frustrating"; "a marriage of convenience"; and "a push-me-pull-you."

This experience of sharing clergy among otherwise separate parishes is set to continue. The Diocese of Bristol is committed, largely on financial grounds, to a strategy which requires the reduction of the number of stipendiary parochial clergy in the diocese by over 20 percent by 2010. No church closures have been envisaged. Whilst, as yet, there have been no decisions taken formally, it seems likely that in the near future a neighbouring parish will be included with the benefice in the allocation of ministerial resources, and that in the medium term the benefice will form two of around seven parishes sharing ministerial resources.

## Pressure from Society

Without wanting to enter the debates about the role of secularisation in the United Kingdom,[7] it is true to say that church attendance is a minority sport. In a city such as Bristol, parish boundaries have little influence on where people

---

6   The staff meeting is open to all licensed ministers within the benefice and in practice attended regularly by the vicar, curate, two licensed readers, and a youth worker. Others attend as their commitments permit. Notes of the meeting are sent to all members of the ministry team, the church wardens of the two parishes, and the benefice administrator. The administrator is the only nonministerial person who has any day-to-day experience of the benefice.

7   For an assessment of different theories of secularisation, see Timothy Jenkins, *Religion in Everyday English Life: An Ethnographic Approach* (New York and Oxford: Berghahn, 1999), 23–39.

attend church. In both parishes the majority of the Sunday congregation live outside the parish boundaries, and this is unremarkable. These churches are chosen by the congregation for a number of reasons. For some it is an issue of churchmanship—both churches fall in between the extremes of evangelical and Anglo-catholic practices which are seen in neighbouring parishes. For others it is because they have found the community to be welcoming to them. Both churches have a policy of welcoming gay and lesbian people. Historical links of churchgoing are also important. St. Paul's has many members who are former students of the University and have continued to worship at St. Paul's after graduation. Many people travel to church at Cotham long after they have left the parish.

Other more widespread changes in society have an effect on the parishes. The increase in house prices, a particularly acute issue in the areas of Bristol served by the two parishes, has led to an increase in multioccupancy houses in the area. People in such accommodation are rarely long-term residents. The increase in mobility and in the dispersion of families across the country combined with the rise in leisure activities makes Sunday morning church-going part of a competitive "market." What constitutes "regular attendance" at church is more likely to be once a month than once a week.

The role of the occasional offices (baptisms, marriages, and funerals) as a point of contact with the wider community are negligible. In 2003, there were five baptisms, five weddings, and five funerals in the benefice.[8] Demographic trends, linked with the increasing value of property in the parishes, explain some of this. However, particularly in terms of the low number of funerals in either church (or at the crematorium), it is clear that for many, perhaps most, of the local population the parish church is no longer a feature of their lives. People resident in the parishes no longer look to the parish church as an integral part of their rites of passage. This is not a pattern that is repeated throughout Bristol, and a combination of economic prosperity and fluid patterns of employment in Cotham and the lack of residential accommodation in St. Paul's parish are significant in explaining the peculiarities of this relationship with the communities in which they are set. Indeed, to speak of "community" at all in these areas starts to beg some difficult questions.

The pressure brought to bear on the parishes of the benefice from the society in which they are set is that the churches will become increasingly irrelevant to that society. One particularly good example of this is the way the two churches minister to residential homes for the elderly. There are five such institutions in the parishes and four are regularly visited by clergy or laity. In each, a notable decline is being detected in the numbers wanting traditional patterns of ministry and those wanting to receive the sacrament of

---

8 These break down in the following way: St Paul's: one baptism, four weddings, no funerals. Cotham: four baptisms, one wedding, five funerals. Of these five funerals, three were taken by clergy from outside the benefice ministry team and one other was a memorial service held at the same time as a funeral took place in Denmark.

Holy Communion. Here we can see that even people in their sixties and seventies are part of a wider social trend that has little or no abiding connection with the church. Such experiences can only increase.

Other forms of engagement with the community go on at both churches. Cotham runs an open drop-in group for carers and children. St. Paul's has a long-established link with the University chaplaincy, which used to run out of the church. Both also let their halls to community groups.

Alternative worship such as the Easter vigil, focused particularly at Cotham, seeks to serve a constituency that comes from across the city and even beyond it. A service in November 2004 brought about eighty people from all over Bristol to worship. Some were habitual churchgoers elsewhere in the city. Many were "dechurched" people, who had stopped going to church but who continue to call themselves Christian.[9] This brings an engagement with society outside the church in a wider sense to more parochially focused work, attempting to engage culturally with "postmodern" and consumerist trends.

These are important ways in which the churches seek to serve and engage with their surrounding communities. Both churches continue to rethink the ways in which their mission and ministry can deepen this engagement. Both continue to be shaped by their encounters, and by the way in which they struggle to make these encounters possible.

## Pressure from Within

Pressure for change from within is of a different nature than the external pressures I have already identified. It comes from various sources, is often contradictory in nature, and there are various timescales attached to it. Some are reactive to changes forced upon or foreseen as coming. Others are more concerned with the type of church people would like to belong to. But there are ideas and initiatives that arise from individuals and groups. The Parochial Church Councils (PCCs) of the parishes are places where some of these ideas are discussed and decided upon. Cotham PCC has spent a good deal of time dealing with issues of how it welcomes people into the community. For a time this found a focus in proposals for changes to the church building, but now it is more concerned with building relationships within the church community and with those in the wider community. Recently, therefore, with the support of the PCC, a series of small groups known as Transforming Communities[10] have been set up. These have two aims. The first is "to build people of Christian

---

9  On "dechurched" people, see Philip Richter and Leslie Francis, *Gone but Not Forgotten* (London: Darton, Longman and Todd, 1998). Richter and Francis suggest that the dechurched make up 40 percent of the population of England. They divide them into the "open" and the "closed" dechurched, depending on their continuing attitudes to the church. This analysis has been very influential in current thinking within the Church of England. See, for example, the General Synod report *Mission Shaped Church: Church Planting and Fresh Expressions of Church in a Changing Context* (London: Church House Publishing, 2004), 36–40.

10  These are consciously modelled on Steven Croft, *Transforming Communities: Re-imagining the Church for the 21st Century* (London: Darton, Longman & Todd, 2002).

faith by strengthening relationships, deepening prayer and worship, growing in the knowledge of the Bible and the Christian tradition, and by enabling and supporting participation in mission and evangelism." The second is "to help us to meet the challenges and opportunities of changes within the church and in the wider society that we seek to serve."[11]

St. Paul's, similarly, has found a focus on building relationships to be crucial. In 2003 St. Paul's celebrated their 150th anniversary, and a forward-looking focus was achieved through a series of "150+ groups" which considered where the church should go in the future. High on this list was the setting up of small groups in order to deepen relationships and explore matters of faith together. In October 2004, a series of Emmaus groups was launched.

But as my story of how we lost our flower arranger shows, the effect of external pressure is often to reveal internal tension. The effect of pressures from the diocese has been to change the relationship between the clergy and the congregations of the benefice. Clergy are no longer experienced as constant features of a church, but are seen roughly fortnightly. A greater division between clergy and congregation is introduced as a result, deepened by the sense that the loyalties of the clergy are at least partly divided between the parishes. Pastoral work is increasingly performed by lay people, whilst the (primarily eucharistic) worship of the churches continues to depend on clergy, but as a class rather than as individuals.

Worship too is an area that both churches are reexamining. Current patterns of eucharistic worship do not appear to be sustainable in the light of declining numbers of clergy. Yet these patterns are carefully constructed compromises between different interests and different preferences within the churches. To take the example of music, St. Paul's has an auditioning choir, largely made up of university students, but this choral tradition does not sit well with children and young people in the congregation or their parents. Some members of Cotham have a strong aversion to choirs in any form, whilst at the same time demands can be heard that we learn new music. The compromises of each church are being opened up for scrutiny.

## What Shapes the Church?

Pressures are a constant feature of the lives of churches. At a time of transition, such as the present one, the pressures are felt more acutely. Old accommodations are no longer possible; new ways of operating must be found. Pressure from the church is felt most from the diocesan, rather than the national or international level. This, in part, reflects the tension within the ecclesiology of the Church of England between episcopal and congregational models. Martyn

---

11 Paper to Cotham PCC, March 2004.

Percy speaks of a "creeping congregationalism" coming into the Church of England,[12] created not least by changing financial arrangements. The diocesan movement towards multiparish arrangements (whether formalised as benefices or not) reinforces the shift towards congregationalism by treating congregations as sacrosanct. Yet at the same time, it is the *diocese* that is calling the tune. Wherever the balance of power will lie in the future, it is certainly being renegotiated.

Pressure from society is felt by the strengthening of the distinction between the church and the wider society. Again in relation to funding, Percy speaks of the change wrought by the way "a comprehensive national ministry is now funded by *congregations* rather than its parishes."[13] It is clear the parish system, understood as the clear identification of a parish church with a bounded geographical area, is simply irrelevant to many both within the congregation and within wider society. Yet at the same time, the clearly established legal and organisational basis provided by the parish system continues to have a huge impact on where the churches choose to engage in mission and ministry. It is still largely to those within the parishes that service is offered.

All of this has the effect of bringing to light internal pressures. Much of this is due to the changing relationship between clergy and congregation. Due to competing pressures for time and attention, the clergy are no longer able to occupy the same role within the congregation. Yet they remain an important part of the church community. How roles and expectations are negotiated between stipendiary clergy, nonstipendiary clergy, congregations, and lay ministers will be of vital importance as change progresses.

Of course, all of this has been simply a reflection by one of the participants in the transition about which I have been speaking. The various stories that can be seen in our Easter vigil service have one thing in common—they are all focussed on the worship of God. This is not worship despite the various pressures that I have identified in this paper, but rather worship which takes place as all these pressures become the stories of the people of God in two parish churches, seeking in faith to follow their Lord.

---

12  Martyn Percy, *The Salt of the Earth: Religious Resilience in a Secular Age* (London and New York: Continuum, 2002), 340.

13  Martyn Percy, "The Priest-like Task: Funding the Ministry of the Church of England," in *The Character of Wisdom: Essays in Honour of Wesley Carr*, ed. Martyn Percy and Stephen Lowe (Aldershot: Ashgate, 2004), 3–21, quotation from p. 3.

# 9

# MINISTRY IN OCCUPATIONAL TRANSFORMATION

## Challenges and Opportunities for the Church in a Time of Trial

*Paula Nesbitt*

At a small gathering of Anglicans across three continents in 2011, members of a U.S. Episcopal diocese shared their projected trends in net income, assets, membership, and average Sunday attendance based on data from the preceeding years. The Africans expressed great dismay at the slow but all-too-steady declines in income, members, and attendance. Those from England nodded solemnly, understanding what the trend indicators shared in common with their own context. Participants discussed the implications affecting funds available for global mission—especially for partnership dioceses that had come to expect and depend on resources for building churches, schools, and other basic infrastructure, education, and exchange opportunities for young, talented clergy. The English participants shared their fiscal dilemma, facing a shift from endowment dependency to a fundraising and development model of self-support. Discussion turned to the frustrations of trying to cultivate a cultural shift toward a stewardship of generosity in the midst of contemporary pressures of consumerism and widespread assumptions that the Church of England, its buildings, its clergy, and overall presence somehow would be maintained without personal support.

This brief interaction symptomized a nexus of issues that face churches in the Anglican Communion, particularly in Westernized locations: growing cultural disengagement and declining participation in mainline religious organizations despite widespread interest in spirituality or religious phenomena (cf. Kosmin and Keysar 2008), declines in fiscal resources, and the implications these and related concerns hold for religious leadership and community, as well as church and communities elsewhere that have depended on support for religious mission and related local needs. These issues form a significant challenge to the structure of many of the autonomous member churches that form the Anglican Communion, as well as the Communion itself.

One of the significant areas where such change has been most visible is in the role of religious leadership among Anglican clergy and laity. The ordained ministry has been in the midst of substantial occupational and organizational change over the last fifty years, as have the role of the laity, partly in response to economic shifts but also in relation to widespread transformations affecting both church and society. This chapter argues that while such alterations involve the meaning and role of ordination itself in church leadership, it also holds deeper implications for the democracy of professional leadership responsible for guiding the development of social cohesion through shared worship, moral reflection, social action, and ultimately Anglican identity.

## Ordained Ministry as Vocation and Occupation

It can be argued that ministry has been undergoing occupational transformation since the very early church. Pauline epistles and the book of Acts illustrate attempts to create occupational order and structure in relation to loosely organized networks of churches with divergent needs and conflicting views of how ministry should be operationalized. The development of specific roles, professionalized specialties, and ordained orders over time was part of this process, typifying what Sociologist Max Weber (1991) argued as the development and eventual professionalization of a leadership class as inevitable to the institutional longevity of a religion.

In Anglican tradition, ordained ministry continued the threefold ordained orders of deacon, priest, and bishop that had come to be widely recognized by the end of the fourth century, but it has focused on priesthood and the episcopate as professional leadership set within the context of apostolic succession. The English Reformation put significant focus on restructuring the priesthood, emphasizing the inseparability of religious vocation from its intimate involvement with congregational life and leadership (Webster 1988). Thus, an apostolic priesthood balanced ministerial charges of both proclaiming the Word and Sacramental leadership (Terwilliger 1975). Subsequent Anglican Reform and Anglo-Catholic movements passionately argued for the dominance of Word or Sacramental aspects, evident in the development of their Anglican theologies of ministry (cf. Hanson 1975, Webster 1988). While Reform perspectives tended to view orders as pragmatically needed for perfection of the church, Anglo-Catholic theologies of ministry eloquently articulated apostolic succession as ground for their authenticity and consequent legitimacy. Yet both affirmed the clergy as constituting Anglicanism's core professional leadership and workforce.

**Ministry as occupation.** The ordained ministry in Anglican and Protestant contexts has consisted of a dialectical relationship of the sacred and secular means by which clergy have understood and enacted their careers within a church structure. The sacred aspect has focused on vocational discernment to which a perceived calling is validated by the church prior to access to ordination and deployment in its organizational structure. Some denominations such as Anglicanism regulate this process through the diocesan or regional level, while some Protestant denominations focus this process within the congregation, although additional denominational requirements often need to be met if one's ordination is to be recognized outside the congregation. This explicit test of a vocational call typically has set apart the clergy from secular occupations, although ascetic Protestantism extended the concept theologically to secular work and activity (Weber 1991, cf. Weber 1958). Concurrently, clergy have been subject to the sociological exigencies of occupational market supply and demand forces, whereby there are a given number of available positions that offer opportunities to exercise one's ministry in an organizational and economically compensated manner. Compensation historically has allowed clergy to specialize in their ministry, ideally full-time, without concurrently needing to hold secular employment.

The traditional norm of clergy expected to commit themselves full-time to their vocation has been operationalized in the life of the church primarily through positions of bishop, cathedral dean, parish rector, vicar, curate, or diocesan staff such as archdeacon or canon. Anglican ordination traditionally has emphasized the close relationship between the office and the congregation (Webster 1988). As an established church, Church of England priests theoretically have been expected to look after the spiritual and, to some extent, physical welfare of those living within their parish boundaries, not just the gathered community of practicing Anglicans (Edwards 1980:340). In disestablished contexts such as the U.S. Episcopal Church, priestly roles have been largely limited to those who voluntarily affiliate with a particular parish congregation (Edwards 1980:340). The extent to which priests concurrently have represented a civic or prophetic voice in community and national affairs has been controversial, embodying larger tensions between the pastoral role of serving the organization and its practicing members, influenced by economic dependency upon a congregation or the church for one's livelihood, and a publicly prophetic role, which can put that dependency relationship at risk (cf. Weber 1991).

The emergence of a single, full-time paid rectorship as normative for the Anglican priesthood was associated with the development of a middle-class clergy in the nineteenth century. Previously, clergy had been sharply stratified. Those with access to good or elite education, and independent financial means, were more likely to secure higher paid positions through patronage or their scholarly achievement, while those with limited education and financial means typically struggled economically, often serving two or more parishes while family members concurrently contributed needed income to the household (Russell 1980, Larson 1977, Holmes 1971). For example, as Russell (1980:30) describes, "The curate of Lastingham in the early eighteenth century had thirteen children to support on a stipend of £20." A survey during that period shows that about half of the positions of that era paid less than £80 annually, with many curacies paying less than £12 (Russell 1980:30–31).

Russell (1980) argues that contributing factors to the eighteenth-century development of a middle-class clergy included wider forces of industrialization and urbanization, as well as both evangelical and Tractarian movements articulating in their own ways a distinctive, specialized role for clergy, which fed a growing self-consciousness of the clergy as a distinct profession, alongside other emergent professions such as law and medicine (cf. Larson 1977). Clergy viewed the other emerging professions as a reference group and model for their own professionalizing development (Edwards 1988). Professionalization steps during this period included greater organizational oversight and control over ministerial formation and requirements for ordination, formalized religious and seminary training that present a distinctive body of knowledge, the development of a discrete clergy subculture and peer networks, and enhanced occupational status through collective expectations of appropriate compensation for services.

Non-elite clergy particularly benefited from occupational professionalization, gaining access to better formal education and enhanced economic status. Realistically, sizable status and income differences remained, but the obligation of one's professional calling ostensibly created a shared bond across class differences. Access to seminary education remained a powerful tool of upward mobility and played a crucial role in the formation of both a broad clerical middle class (Holmes 1971:97) and the development of normative clerical positions and role expectations for them.

## Roots of Contemporary Occupational Transformations

A detailed analysis would reveal numerous times of trial that Anglicanism and its clergy have faced, from a widespread apathy toward religion in the eighteenth century to the intense ideological debates over the proper understanding of the church and its clergy a century later. The North American context differed markedly, as both the Canadian and the American churches contended not only with serving immigrant Anglicans but also an emergent competitive religious marketplace. In the U.S. the development of a denomination, an Anglican identity, and a polity distinct from the Church of England also represented a significant transformation for both clergy and laity. Such factors tended to mitigate to some extent the effects of English ecclesial stresses. Additionally, clergy willing to serve rural and frontier areas continued to face sharply different socioeconomic realities than those in the wealthy urban centers, which also delayed the development of a cohesive professional clergy class for a number of years. By the latter nineteenth century, developments in theological education as well as greater access to seminary training resulted in a growing professional clerical class consciousness among clergy within mainline denominations, but also a felt erosion of civic and public presence within what Douglas (1977) articulated as a privatized professional role that shared many feminized characteristics of Victorian culture of that era.

Citing Tocqueville's observation that both ministers and women held authority only within the domestic and personal spheres, Douglas (1977) argues that the disenfranchisement of religion from the U.S. state resulted in economic dependency on local congregations that hindered both the public authoritative and persuasive power that clergy held on topics of public interest during the colonial era. The combination of social pressure and economic leverage that laity developed over clergy also resulted in focusing clerical roles on the privatized religious sphere of pastoral relationship and care. Clergy, like women of the era, came to be held to high moral ideals and behavioral standards that typically differed from traits associated with masculine virility. Obligatory virtue became situated in a minister's character rather than in the professional role that once fortified the occupation with its distinct power and privilege. Douglas (1977) also points to a deprofessionalization trend embedded within liberal Protestantism, ensuing from the occupational split between the theological and pastoral dimensions of ministry, which by the mid-nineteenth century was exacerbated by a growing trend toward anti-institutionalism that further eroded clergy prestige. A notable exception to this erosion involved clergy ministering to racially segregated and marginalized congregations, and developing frontier communities, where opportunities for some public and prophetic leadership (understood within the context of Weber's [1978] office charisma) continued.

## Twentieth-Century Challenges in the American Context

Stemming from the legacy of the ordained clergy articulated as both religious vocation and occupational profession, as well as contributing socio-cultural trends such as Douglas' (1977) feminization thesis and ensuing movements seeking to restore a masculinized vitality to the clergy (Douglas 1977, cf. Bendroth 1992), several challenges to the clergy in the contemporary American church over the past fifty years have contributed to the contemporary dilemma in the twenty-first century. They have had a strong impact on the clergy, and to a sizable extent on Anglicanism overall. I will focus on three: the ordination of women and subsequently openly gay clergy, shifting understandings of vocational identity, and occupational deprofessionalization. These are set against a backdrop of declining economic resources that historically have supported the denominational structure with a professional clergy.

The debate on women's ordination, by the late 1960s, had begun to create serious reflexivity on the nature of ordained ministry and whether or not it was contingent on one's gender. The U.S. Episcopal Church granted women ordination to the diaconate at its 1970 General Convention, with priesthood failing only in the clergy vote. In 1971, women were granted ordination to the priesthood in Hong Kong, Macao, and Kenya. By 1973, a sizable backlash emerged to opening the priesthood to women, which led to a more focused examination on the nature of priesthood among those on both sides of the issue (e.g., Hewitt and Hiatt 1973, Terwilliger and Holmes 1975). Some urged the need for greater clarity on both a doctrine of priesthood and on human sexuality (e.g., Allin 1975: vii). For some this was partly to challenge expressed anxieties such that the prospect of female priests would sexually tempt male clergy, cause male impotency, or that menstruating women would contaminate the sacraments (Hewitt and Hiatt 1973, Carmody 1979, Huyck 1981). Other concerns centered on a feminization thesis: that women would take over the ordained ministry as well as lay church work, causing men to leave both the occupation and the church. For those who remained, both occupational prestige and compensation would vastly diminish (cf. Nesbitt 1997).

Following the 1976 regularization of women's ordination to the priesthood, the absence of young men from the ordination process became particularly evident by the mid-1980s, which followed a trend in other mainline denominations that ordained women, but also showed some similarities to the supply dislocations of young male clerics in the Catholic Church (Nesbitt 1997; cf. Schoenherr and Young 1993) where female clergy were not a contributing factor. Concurrent trends among Episcopal clergy during that era showed a rising age at ordination, a growing prevalence of part-time parish placements and in nonparochial positions, and proportionally fewer senior leadership opportunities. These trends, however, had begun to appear in the 1960s, and particularly in unfolding careers of men ordained in 1970, well prior to the presence of female priests, according to a longitudinal study of Episcopal male and female clergy (Nesbitt 1997; cf. Gustafson 1965). An aging trend had been identified among newly ordained clergy in the Church of England in the 1950s (Wilson 1969) as well. Elsewhere I have argued that the entry of women into the clergy effectively served as an alternative labor supply to disproportionately fill positions that were lower-paid, part-time, or nonstipendiary, and that an increased ratio of female clergy has a direct effect on the concentration of men in positions offering higher status and attainment (Nesbitt 1997).

While the ordination of openly gay clergy has not been a significant issue so long as they were celibate, pressures to legitimize gay and lesbian clergy living in partnered relationships began shortly after women were granted ordination to the priesthood (Sumner 1987). In the intervening years, some bishops openly ordained them without enforcing celibacy, but it would take thirty years for the Episcopal Church to formalize a position analogous to women's ordination, where ordination decisions were left to individual dioceses. As with female clergy, the occupational opportunities of openly gay clergy have varied by dioceses and parishes willing to consider their leadership. One study on Episcopal clergy did show that single male clergy (not having been heterosexually married) were significantly less likely to attain rectorships or equivalent positions than their married counterparts (Nesbitt

1995). Thus, presence of gay clergy, as with female clergy, likely contributed to the enhanced occupational status of heterosexually married male clergy.

Second, some contended that a mid-century crisis in ministry was also linked to broader concerns of vocational identity. Blizzard's (1985 [1956]) study of role fragmentation and other studies of conflict and change in vocational self-understanding, predating the intensity of debate over women's ordination, suggested that the issue perhaps became a focal point in a much larger and deeper vocational crisis (e.g., Terwilliger and Holmes 1975). Others saw the dilemma as a growing occupational confusion, where the priesthood had become separated from its purpose, resulting in an erosion of occupational authority. This was said to have occurred through associating Christian priesthood with Old Testament understandings of priesthood, resulting in a loss of focus on serving the gospel, an overly narrow emphasis on validity criteria for ordination, a preoccupation with credentials, and an avoidance of doctrinal clarity despite ordination vows to uphold the doctrine and discipline of the church (Allison 1975). This was further illustrated in a long-standing confusion in the church over what to call a priest which, it was argued, illustrated a wider perplexity over ministry itself. This naming dilemma only became exacerbated as ordained women entered congregational ministry and faced uncertainty and resistance over how they should be addressed (Allison 1975). The occupational confusion thesis also has affected clergy in the Church of England as well as the U.S. Episcopal Church.

A third challenge has been a related transition from a self-understanding of clergy as set apart, through ordination rites and apostolic succession, as well as professionalized training and role specialization, to an understanding of clergy as enabling or facilitating the ministry of the entire Body of Christ (cf. Kleinman 1984). Evidence of this transition had become visible around 1970, according to Kleinman (1984), and logically resulted in confusion over what was professionally distinctive to the ordained ministry that couldn't be done by laity. The ultimate conclusion, if clergy were successful, would be to work themselves out of a professional role and parish position. This was particularly problematic for Protestant clergy from nonsacramental denominations or where ritual acts such as baptism or communion were not limited to ordained ministers.

For clergy in sacramental denominations such as the Episcopal Church, this led to a narrowing focus in vocational discernment to identify those who articulated their call as one to perform distinct sacramental acts: namely Eucharist and reconciliation. The professionalization and growth of the diaconate as a distinct order during the 1970s and 1980s, idealized as grounded in nonstipendiary service, has further confounded what was professionally distinctive to priesthood beyond these two sacramental acts. Additionally, growing lay ministry movements during this period challenged traditional notions of clergy professionalization and role specialization (e.g., Rowthorn 1986).

The deprofessionalization thesis saw its anthesis in growing clericalism through the professionalization of the diaconate, and in professionalizing licensing practices developed for laity to serve as readers, chalice bearers, and other liturgical or parish roles. The professionalization of parish laity has continued while ordination criteria for deacons and priests have become more flexible in terms of educational preparation and background, particularly for those willing to serve in nonstipendiary positions (cf. Nesbitt 1997). While occasionally laity and deacons serve in part-time or full-time paid professional ministry positions, compensated ministry normally has continued to be limited to the priesthood. Thus, what has remained sociologically distinctive for the priesthood has been sacramental role specialty and the ability to be paid for one's ministerial work.

## Ministry in Changing Times

Today, although full-time paid parish placements are still the norm for Anglican and Episcopal churches, they have become increasingly less common relative to the number of active priests, even when excluding those not interested in parish ministry. Furthermore, while traditionally the norm for ordained male priests, this has never been the case for women (Nesbitt 1997, Blohm 2005, cf. Zikmund et al. 1998). Rather, women have been more likely to hold staff positions and to move laterally into similar positions. From a recent study on Episcopal clergy ("Called to Serve" 2010), which sampled 2,373 clergy overall, men ordained in the 1970s continue to illustrate to a large degree the traditional normative model for priesthood careers in earlier decades (Figure 1). For men ordained in the 1980s and subsequently, the percentage of those ever having held a rectorship or vicarship drops significantly. Averaging the trendlines for both men and women, a marked downward shift over the last four decades becomes evident. Ironically the gender gap continues to remain constant since women's ordination in the 1970s.

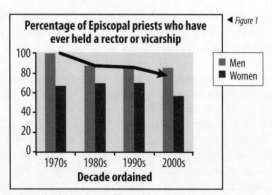

◀ *Figure 1*

Source: "Called to Serve," survey of Episcopal clergy, CPG et al. 2009.

Figure 2 compares those having held rectorships by age at ordination, which shows that rising average age at ordination does not explain the overall decline in clergy who have held rectorships. Furthermore, women were significantly less likely than men in every age category below sixty to have held a rectorship. Although it has been argued that women have less interest in such positions, given disproportionate responsibilities for family care, limitations on geographic mobility, or not wanting the demands of such a position, women were 25 percent more likely to have applied for such positions but never held one than men. This was especially so for women ordained in their twenties and thirties, compared to men the same age.

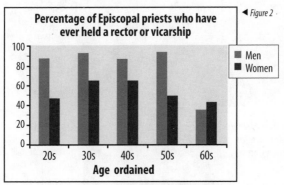

Source: "Called to Serve," survey of Episcopal clergy, CPG et al. 2009.

Declines in active church membership, economic recession, and unemployment that have affected most middle class parishes, and high costs associated with buildings and their maintenance, combined with standardized norms for clergy compensation and tight diocesan budgets that have limited institutional subsidies for poorer congregations, have resulted in parish mergers, closures, and small, struggling parishes becoming yoked together into cluster ministries. Some clergy hold multipoint charges that may involve serving two, three, or as many as ten churches, often across a substantial distance. Although the latter has been characteristic of rural ministries for centuries, the growing prevalence in urban and suburban areas is a much more recent trend. According to the "Called to Serve" data, of priests engaged in parish ministry, about 10 percent serve more than one parish concurrently.

Proportionally more clergy have been ministering in part-time, quarter-time, or nonstipendiary positions than fifty years ago (cf. Nesbitt 1997). Figure 3 shows clergy interest in holding full-time and other positions, despite the type of placement that they might currently have, suggesting that female priests have a strong interest in full-time work. It also is important to note the strong interest in paid work by deacons, despite a professionalized articulation of the diaconate as a nonstipendiary role. The data showed that 60 percent of deacons, who in this data set are 99 percent female, preferred some kind of stipendiary arrangement for their ministries. In other tests, the data show that half of the deacons in the study work more than forty hours monthly.

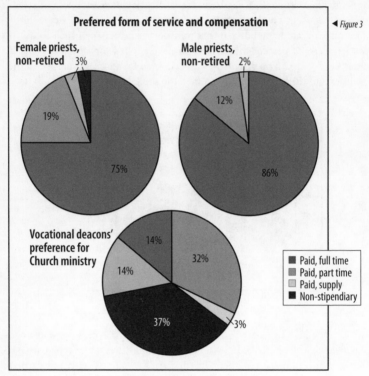

**Preferred form of service and compensation** ◀ *Figure 3*

Source: "Called to Serve," survey of Episcopal clergy, CPG et al. 2009.

Of clergy who hold nonstipendiary parish placements, women are significantly more likely than men to also have paid work outside the parish, which suggests that nonstipendiary status may be a retirement vocation for men but a balance of paid work and unpaid ministry for women, according to the "Called to Serve" study (Figure 4). Women are much more likely to hold a part-time placement as well as work outside the parish. Also significant is the high percentage of both men and women who work full-time in the parish but also work for pay elsewhere, suggesting that there may be some need for additional compensation beyond what parishes are able to pay.

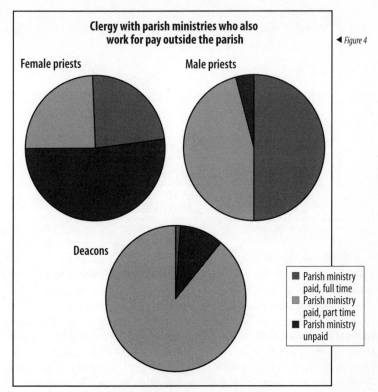

Source: "Called to Serve," survey of Episcopal clergy, CPG et al. 2009.

Consequently, the normative position of a paid full-time priest responsible for a self-supporting parish is both becoming less common but also potentially more competitive in who ultimately is called or hired to such positions. Given the increasingly diverse demographics of clergy today, particularly in gender and amount of adult lay experience prior to ordination, potential competition for proportionally fewer full-time, paid placements in parish and diocesan staffs raises fresh concerns about the potential for the restratified growth of elitism within the clergy.

Furthermore, the "Called to Serve" data show that female priests tend to commit more hours to nonstipendiary ministries than men (Figure 5), despite evidence that they are more likely to hold paid work outside the parish (cf. Figure 4).

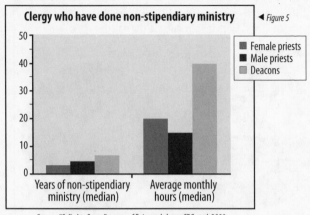

Source: "Called to Serve," survey of Episcopal clergy, CPG et al. 2009.

In the "Called to Serve" study, when clergy were asked about interest in non-traditional models of ministry, namely those other than full-time parish work, we see that other types of ministry tend to be valued less by male priests than by female priests or deacons (Figure 6). Female priests in the "Called to Serve" study consistently showed a greater openness to different forms of paid and nonpaid ministries. Given women's greater family caregiving responsibilities, this flexibility may reflect an interest in the availability of nontraditional ministries at difference life stages. This suggests that men may feel less concerned about the need to consider nontraditional ministry options. Furthermore, the lukewarm interest by all clergy for nontraditional placements, when combined with a constriction of paid placements, raises additional questions over the extent to which both the church and the clergy are willing to embrace nontraditional, bivocational, and collaborative models of ministry as both legitimate and worthy of professional esteem and status.

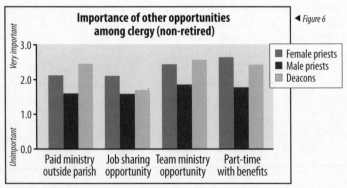

Source: "Called to Serve," survey of Episcopal clergy, CPG et al. 2009.

Not surprisingly, nonparochial or nonstipendiary priests have been regarded skeptically, particularly as proportionally more male clergy in the 1970s moved into such placements (Nesbitt 1997). Rectors, deployment officers, and others working with clergy transitions often have characterized them as unfit or unable to hold stipendiary positions, or as "loose cannons" who should not have the same voice and vote as parochial clergy (Nesbitt 1997:157, Lowery 1988). Female priests have been disproportionately concentrated in nonparochial and nonstipendiary ministries, stemming from their greater difficulty in geographic mobility, greater vulnerability to forced mobility through their greater likelihood to hold staff positions, which can be more easily abolished when budgets are tight or can be subject to conflicts with a new or ongoing rector. Nonstipendiary positions can be a means of remaining active in ministry while seeking or being called to a paid cure (Price and Nesbitt 2010, Nesbitt 1997). However, the question of whether nontraditional and nonstipendiary priesthood ministries are legitimated such that they are evenly distributed across gender and other demographic characteristics is important. Significantly, given the vast amount of time contributed through nonstipendiary ministries, of the 25 percent of nonretired men who have done nonstipendiary ministry, virtually none preferred it. Few women preferred it as well. However, given the likelihood of more nonstipendiary ministry in the church's future, an important challenge remains to make it more acceptable if not altogether desirable.

## Conclusion

While in some ways unsettling, the "Called to Serve" data show that clergy have some resources for alternative models of ministry that allow them to consider their vocation and their ministry creatively, beyond where those currently not in the pews might be, while still attending to traditional priestly roles and responsibilities. It also raises further questions over the boundaries of professional ministry, particularly the occupational role of the priesthood beyond the parish and how an Anglican theology of ministry can be articulated to embrace widened options and opportunities. There also appears to be a small but slightly growing interest in doing so, particularly among female priests and deacons. However, if occupational market forces prevail, the data suggest there is a strong likelihood of a reemergence of a two-tier clergy: a small elite core that is primarily male who hold traditional full-time paid parish rectorships and elite leadership positions, while other clergy minister on the margin trying to make economic ends meet, perhaps not unreminiscent of the eighteenth-century curate of Lastingham (Russell 1980). Alternatively, the U.S. Episcopal Church and its clergy are at an important decision point in how resources are shared so that one another's ministries are supported across the church. Such resources aren't limited to compensation, but also include a valuation and commitment to a diversity of forms and seeking ways to make them viable. Given tight economic pressures and constraints, the Anglican Church of Canada shares such concerns, with perhaps long-term relevance for the Church of England to consider as well.

In conclusion, the current time of trial is most explicitly characterized by declining economic resources that hold implications for the continuance of a middle-class and professionalized clergy. The challenges involve the risk of a growing clerical elistism, with increasing status differences, systemic demographic inequalities with sizable gender cleavages, as well as traditional class disparities and potential disruption in focused ministerial efforts as more clergy as well as laity engage as "tentmakers," while holding other employment. Yet opportunities also include creative rethinking of what church ministry might involve, sharing resources in fresh ways, and a growing democratization of ministerial forms and the vocation overall, giving more clergy freedom to explore new forms of ministry that are regarded as both politically legitimate and of value. Attendant to this are the opportunities to revisit Anglican theological understandings of ministry and their societal applications that extend beyond building walls and those most comfortable within them.

# References

Allin, John Maury. 1975. "Forward." In *To Be A Priest: Perspectives on Vocation and Ordination,* edited by Robert E. Terwilliger and Urban T. Holmes, III, vii–viii. New York: Crossroad Books, Seabury Press.

Allison, C. FitzSimons. 1975. "What Is a Priest? Another Anglican View." In Terwilliger and Holmes, eds., *To Be A Priest,* 11–19.

Bendroth, Margaret Lamberts. 1992. "Fundamentalism and Femininity: Points of Encounter Between Religious Conservatives and Women, 1919–1935." *Church History* 61: 221–33.

Blizzard, Samuel. 1985 [1956]. *The Protestant Minister: A Behavioral Science Interpretation.* Society for the Scientific Study of Religion Monograph Series, No. 5. Storrs, CT: Society for the Scientific Study of Religion.

Blohm, Uta. 2005. *Religious Traditions and Personal Stories: Women Working as Priests, Ministers and Rabbis.* Frankfurt: Peter Lang.

"Called to Serve." 2010. A Study of Clergy Careers, Clergy Wellness, and Clergy Women. Jointly sponsored by: the Executive Council's Committee on the Status of Women, The Church Pension Fund's Office of Research, The Episcopal Church Center's Office of Women's Ministry, and CREDO Institute, Inc. http://www.cpg.org.

Carmody, Denise L. 1979. *Women and World Religions.* Nashville: Abingdon Press.

Douglas, Ann. 1977. *The Feminization of American Culture.* New York: Alfred A. Knopf.

Edwards, O. C. Jr. 1988. "Anglican Pastoral Tradition." In *The Study of Anglicanism,* edited by Stephen Sykes and John Booty, 338–51. London: SPCK/Fortress Press.

Gustafson, J. M. 1965. "The Clergy in the United States." In *The Professions in America,* edited by K. S. Lynn and the editors of *Daedalus,* 70–90. Boston: Houghton Mifflin.

Hanson, Anthony. 1975. *Church, Sacraments and Ministry.* London and Oxford: Mowbrays.

Hewitt, Emily C., and Suzanne R. Hiatt. 1973. *Women Priests: Yes or No?* New York: Seabury Press.

Heyer, R. J., ed. *Women and Orders.* New York: Paulist Press, 1974.

Holmes, Urban T. III. 1971. *The Future Shape of Ministry: A Theological Projection.* New York: Seabury Press.

Huyck, Heather A. 1981. "To Celebrate a Whole Priesthood: The History of Women's Ordination in the Episcopal Church." PhD diss., University of Minnesota.

Kleinman, Sheryl. 1984. *Equals Before God: Seminarians as Humanistic Professionals.* Chicago: University of Chicago Press.

Kosmin, Barry A., and Ariela Keysar. 2009. "American Nones: The Profile of the No Religion Population," American Religious Identification Survey 2008. Hartford, CT: Trinity College, 2009. http://www.americanreligion survey-aris.org/.

Larson, Magali Sarfatti. 1977. *The Rise of Professionalism: A Sociological Analysis.* Berkeley: University of California Press.

Lowery, James L. Jr. 1988. "'Tentmaker Priests' Contend They Have Apostolic Vocation." *The Lambeth Daily* 21 July, 3.

Nesbitt, Paula D. 1995. "Marriage, Parenthood and the Ministry: Differential Effects of Marriage and Family on Male and Female Clergy Careers." *Sociology of Religion* 56 (4): 397–415.

———. 1997. *Feminization of the Clergy in America: Occupational and Organizational Perspectives.* New York: Oxford University Press.

Price, Matthew, and Paula Nesbitt. 2010. "Thirty-five Years of Women Priests: Celebrating Change, Clarifying the Challenges Ahead." *Ruach* Winter: 10–12, 26.

Roof, Wade Clark, and William McKinney. 1987. *American Mainline Religion: Its Changing Shape and Future.* New Brunswick and London: Rutgers University Press.

Rowthorn, Anne. 1986. *The Liberation of the Laity.* Wilton: Morehouse-Barlow.

Russell, Anthony. 1980. *The Clerical Profession.* London: SPCK.

Schoenherr, Richard A., and Lawrence A. Young. 1993. *Full Pews and Empty Altars: Demographics of the Priest Shortage in United States Dioceses.* Madison: University of Wisconsin Press.

Sumner, Donald E. 1987. *The Episcopal Church's History: 1945–1985.* Wilton: Morehouse-Barlow.

Terwilliger, Robert E. 1975. "What Is a Priest? One Anglican View." In Terwilliger and Holmes, eds., *To Be A Priest,* 3–10.

Terwilliger, Robert E., and Urban T. Holmes III. 1975. "Preface." In Terwilliger and Holmes, eds., *To Be A Priest,* ix–x.

———. 1975. *To Be A Priest: Perspectives on Vocation and Ordination.* New York: Crossroad Books, Seabury Press.

Weber, Max. 1958. *The Protestant Ethic and the Spirit of Capitalism.* New York: Charles Scribner's Sons.

———. 1978. *Economy and Society.* Edited by Guenther Roth and Claus Wittich. Vol. 1–2. Berkeley: University of California Press.

———. 1991 [1922]. *The Sociology of Religion.* Translated by Ephraim Fishoff. Introduction by Talcott Parsons. Boston: Beacon Press.

Webster, John B. 1988. "Ministry and Priesthood." In Sykes and Booty, eds., *The Study of Anglicanism,* 285–96.

Wilson, B. R. 1969. *Religion in Secular Society.* Baltimore: Penguin Books.

Zikmund, Barbara Brown, Adair T. Lummis, and Patricia M. Y. Chang. 1998. *Clergy Women: An Uphill Calling.* Louisville, KY: Westminster/John Knox Press.

# 10

# A (STRANGE) SORT OF HOMECOMING?

## Anglicanorum Coetibus and the Ecumenical Responsibilities of Contemporary Anglicans and Roman Catholics[1]

*Gerard Mannion*

### Strife in the Anglican Communion

Numerous scholars and commentators have provided us with accounts of the joys and hopes, the griefs and anguishes of Anglican church communities in recent decades. However, the key moments, trends and debates in this particular part of the church point are indicative of ecclesial changes of much wider relevance, particularly with regard to shifts in the understanding of the church-world dynamic and relationship, the ecclesial retreat 'inwards' from the wider 'world' by many Anglicans in recent times, the move to restore perceived 'traditional' values and aspects of being church, and the denunciation of much of contemporary culture and of all things perceived 'liberal'. The changing notions of mission and evangelisation in these decades are of further relevance here. More specifically, some commentators have focused upon tensions and schismatic forces over questions of sexuality, gender roles, ministry, authority, leadership and the wider ecclesial malaises illustrated by the shadow of colonialism. Others have sought to illustrate as being out of touch the worldviews of many within the church, as well as the theological jousting that has taken place as the backdrop to such developments.

To any Roman Catholic these specific stories sound all too agonisingly familiar. Indeed, for that matter, to any Christian in most parts of the globe, the more general trends identified by the recent travails of Anglicans, as well as numerous aspects of the specific struggles, are equally all too familiar.

---

1   The original version of this paper was composed in the aftermath of the release of *Anglicanorum Coetibus* in 2009. This is an updated version to take into account developments in the period since.

From this we can see the stories of particular Anglican communities in the last five decades or so offer a microcosm of the travails (as well as some of the triumphs, of course) of the wider Christian family. This can be perceived in terms of the concentric circles of the Anglican Communion itself, but equally in terms of the entire church universal. Here the words of Paul Avis, in relation to intra-Anglican divisions, prove instructive, "This is not necessarily unhealthy, a sign of ecclesial pathology. In some ways, the (normal) state of the Christian Church is to be seething with argument and controversy. Conflict is endemic in Christianity and Anglicanism is not a special case."[2]

Many involved in ecclesiological debates today have fruitfully utilised the notion of 'social imaginary', so central to the work of philosophers and social scientists in recent times, most notably Charles Taylor. Other contributions to this volume do so in particular.[3] Ecclesial and moral imaginaries can be understood as part of the broader social imaginaries. What developments within Anglicanism and across the Christian church globally appear to offer today is further evidence that older and more repressive social imaginaries are making a comeback across the church and theology alike—albeit with distinctly postmodern twists. These social imaginaries accentuate otherness in a pejorative sense. Rather than mutuality and interdependence, they perceive difference in a negative light and affirm a retreat from the wider social settings wherein Christians live out their daily forms of existence.

But there is an increasing need today for people to understand and appreciate how we can never really, especially in these times, live according to a single, uniform social imaginary, but rather we live in terms of a series of 'multiple-belongings' and through a mosaic of differing social imaginaries—sometimes complementary, sometimes not. Within the churches the same is also true. We also need to come to a renewed appreciation of unity through diversity, as well as of the sense of catholicity itself, and in qualitative, rather than crudely quantitative terms.

All in all, this suggests that attempts to impose a normative ecclesiology that we see in various churches today, which seek to impose a uniformity of a world-renouncing kind, betray a misunderstanding of what catholicity truly is.[4]

Indeed, recent developments vis-a-vis the Anglican Communion help provide further evidence for the theory that some of us have been putting forward in recent times that we are witnessing something of a 'trans-denominational'

---

2   Paul Avis, 'Anglican Ecclesiology' in *The Routledge Companion to the Christian Church*, Gerard Mannion with Lewis Mudge, Editors (London and New York, Routledge, 2007), 202. Elsewhere I have discussed the necessity, at times, for 'conflictual dialogue', drawing upon the work of Gregory Baum, c.f. Gerard Mannion, *Ecclesiology and Postmodernity—Questions for the Church in our Times* (Collegeville, Michael Glazier, 2007), 142–45.

3   Elsewhere, I have utilized the concept of social imaginary in relation both to the development concerning Roman Catholic attitudes toward sexuality and toward magisterium. See, e.g., 'Magisterium as a Social Imaginary: Contemporary Challenges and Future Ways Forward' in *When the Magisterium Intervenes . . .* ed. Richard R. Gaillardetz, Michael Glazier/Liturgical Press, forthcoming, 2012.

4   I have discussed these developments at greater length elsewhere, 'Postmodern Ecclesiologies', ch. 7 of *The Routledge Companion to the Christian Church*, (Mannion and Mudge, eds., 2007, 127–52) and *Ecclesiology and Postmodernity, passim.*

reformation in the Christian church at present which should equally be under-stood as a series of developments motivated, in the main, by the need to react to the variously perceived ills of postmodernity. That is to say that whereas fundamental differences between Christians (be they in terms of doctrine, ethics, worship and, crucially, ecclesiology) once used to be, primarily, along denominational lines, such is no longer the case. Indeed, it is far more likely today that one can have much more in common with groups of Christians of another denomination than with many within one's own Christian denomi-nation. Hence, in so many ways, the lines of 'division' amongst Christians are thus now trans-denominational rather than inter-denominational (i.e., across rather than between denominations).

Such a 'trans-denominational' reformation has played a significant role in the advent of an ecumenical and inter-faith winter, the decline in dialogical and open theological enquiry and the emergence of new schools of thought, particularly 'reactionary' forms of postmodern theology. What brings about such theological shifts relates to the operative understanding of those afore-mentioned relations between the church and world, as well as upon nature and grace and the ecclesiological implications of both. The advent of a 'neo-exclusivist' form of ecclesial being and forms of understanding that being can be seen across the majority of Christian denominations.[5]

One of the subsequent consequences of this rise in world-renouncing ecclesiologies is that they fuel a return to understanding mission primarily, indeed often solely, in terms of conversion and also seem to associate being faithful to the Gospel with absolutist positions on particular moral issues. This leads to attempts to reject all dissent with regard to the same.

All such developments across the wider Christian family might all offer a way of understanding and explaining recent developments within the Anglican Communion, as well as the decision by numerous Anglicans to seek to join the Roman Catholic Church in a corporate fashion. Developments in recent times concerning intra-Anglican divisions help illustrate how this 'trans-denominational' reformation is gathering pace.

But, of course, among the more recent developments that have gener-ated controversy is the release of the Apostolic Constitution on the 'Anglican Ordinariates' by Pope Benedict XVI in 2009. To this specific development we now turn.

## *Anglicanorum Coetibus:* The Establishment of a Roman Catholic Ordinariate for Anglicans

Given the divisions across the church in these times, Rome's recent and direct intervention into intra-Anglican discord can be seen as, at the very best, inop-portune, taking a generous view that there are sincerely ecumenical intentions

---

5  I explain this thesis concerning neo-exclusivism in more detail in Gerard Mannion, *Ecclesiology and Postmodernity: Questions for the Church in Our Time* (Collegeville, MN., Michael Glazier, 2007), esp. chs. 1–4.

behind the 'Note' released by the Congregation for the Doctrine of the Faith (CDF), prior to the Apostolic Constitution, *Anglicanorum Coetibus*, as well as behind the Constitution and accompanying Norms (signed November 4, 2009). At worst, at the other end of the hermeneutical spectrum, more critical voices would perceive the intervention as an ecumenically irresponsible act that serves nobody in the church entirely well. There was a flurry of commentaries, not all of it well advised or accurate, in the immediate aftermath of the release of these documents.

Some commentators (including a few with books to sell) descended into hyperbole and insulting generalisations about the Roman Catholic Church. Certain other commentators on these events seem to have missed the ecumenical point, focusing upon the development primarily from intra-Roman Catholic perspectives. Such is certainly important, for the impact of *Anglicanorum Coetibus* upon Roman Catholic local, diocesan and national churches is potentially very significant indeed, as we hope to illustrate. But a one-sided focus on, for example, the possible impact of the establishment of Ordinariates upon Roman Catholic episcopal collegiality in certain countries overlooks how quietly many Roman Catholics today, including bishops appointed according to such views, appear to be subsuming a restorationist understanding of ecclesial communion and authority, as well as mission and evangelisation. But the most important significance of these developments concerns the lasting impact upon the evangelically imperatival and necessarily collective search for Christian harmony and communion, so often termed 'unity'. But let us first turn to explore this document itself and its impact within the Roman Catholic Church.

At the time of the release of this document in 2009, prior to the first Anglicans under this initiative being admitted to the Roman Catholic Church and priesthood in 2011,[6] it appeared that this particular move towards 'unity' was being announced well in advance to test the water before the real logistical details were finalised. The developments were said to be taking place in response to approaches from a number of Anglicans directly to Rome. But one vitally significant question which was so glaringly obvious then, as it is now, concerns why the CDF and not the Pontifical Council for Christian Unity dealt with this sensitive issue in the first place. At the time of the release it was widely believed that not only were the Archbishops of Canterbury and (Roman Catholic) Westminster kept in the dark about this document until the Note was released, but so, also was the Cardinal Prefect of the said

---

6  The first received into the Roman Catholic Church under these arrangements were three former Anglican bishops, alongside some of their relatives and three former Anglican women religious, on January 1, 2011, with those bishops being ordained Roman Catholics priests to much fanfare on January 15, 2011. Two additional former Anglican bishops were subsequently ordained as Roman Catholic priests, also. It has been estimated some nine hundred Anglicans joined the Roman Catholic Church as part of the new Ordinariate at Easter in 2011, including some sixty-one clergy (and an additional two former Anglican Bishops). At the time of writing (June 2011), beginning at Pentecost, there have been a series of ordinations of many of these clergy to the Roman Catholic priesthood. The name of the new ordinariate is 'The Personal Ordinariate of Our Lady of Walsingham'.

Pontifical Council. Subsequent reports suggested that Rowan Williams had around two and a half weeks' notice. With regard to the curial office dealing with the entire matter, testimonies from Anglicans who 'crossed the Tiber' (the colloquial expression for Anglicans who become Roman Catholics) suggest that the simple answer was that Cardinal Walter Kasper, the Prefect of the Council for Unity at the time some Anglicans sought conversations in Rome, around 2008, responded that his council dealt only with churches and not groups or individuals within them. Cardinal William Levada, Prefect of the CDF, responded much more enthusiastically.[7]

Let us first turn to examine the actual documents which set in place the means by which these new ecclesial entities will be established, bearing in mind the differing levels of the implications of their being established.

## What's New? *Anglicanorum Coetibus* and the Complementary Norms: Some Hermeneutical Reflections

The Ordinariates themselves are 'erected' by the CDF—not by the requisite national episcopal conference (*Anglicanorum Coetibus* I§1), although the CDF is to establish the ordinariates "in consultation with" the latter in some unspecified form. As in the words of *Anglicanorum Coetibus*, "Each Ordinariate . . . is juridically comparable to a diocese" (I§3), in effect, then, the separatists, sectarian or "people set apart" nature of an Ordinariate would appear to have become enshrined in canon law. Because one can envision, particularly in North America, possibly more than one Ordinariate coming into being in a single country, the notion of a 'diocese' within a diocese is even made possible. The first Ordinariate, established in Britain, reaches across many dioceses. And there are provisions conceivable for a deanery within a deanery, as the Ordinary is able to establish deaneries should he see fit. These are separatist or sectarian trends that have been resisted throughout various stages of the history of the church. Poignantly, when perceived more progressive groups of Roman Catholics have differed with their own local ordinaries in recent decades, their attempts to obtain greater autonomy in the governance of their Christian communities has been forcefully resisted. Yet this 2009 document was released seemingly oblivious to how divisive some reactionary Anglican groups have proved within dioceses and national churches and across the Anglican Communion already. Was it considered that the vociferous objections to their fellow Christians uttered by so many in their

---

7   C.f. John Wilkins, 'With a Thousand Anglican Converts, Ordinariate gets Going', *National Catholic Reporter* (May 23, 2011), http://ncronline.org/news/global/thousand-anglican-converts-ordinariate-gets-going (accessed May 23, 2011). Perhaps some further backdrop to this entire situation might be offered by some of the themes discussed in relation to Archbishop Joseph Ratzinger's understanding of the 'solution' to the 'ecumenical problem' in his *Principles of Catholic Theology: Building Stones for a Fundamental Theology.* (San Francisco: Ignatius, 1987, pp. 193–203). An abbreviated version with commentary is featured in Lieven Boeve and Gerad Mannion (eds.), *The Ratzinger Reader: Mapping a Theological Journey* (New York and London, Continuum), 2010.

113

number will not cease just because they will now be a 'people set apart' from Roman Catholic instead of Anglican neighbours?

Some engaged consultation here would have made such self-evident. (The mention in section V of the Ordinary's potestas being exercised 'jointly' with the local diocesan bishop, remains ambiguous and qualified only by the phrase "in those cases provided for in the Complementary Norms"). VI §4 speaks of further common activities between an Ordinariate and local diocese, but the language makes clear that the two are clearly separate ecclesial entities in the main. They are united, for sure, as all Roman Catholic Christians are united, but not part of one and the same local Christian community, i.e., the body of Christ in this place here and now. §5 makes this clear as even separate seminary programs and houses of formation are thus made possible. The question that this all further raises is why this emphasis upon separatism? Anglican sensibilities and traditions could be respected and integrated in numerous ways without recourse to separatist provisions. It is not as if such Anglicans would be landing from Mars and, of course, given the wonderful achievements of Anglican-Roman Catholic ecumenical efforts in recent years, many seminaries and theological institutions and university departments would have no difficulty at all in accommodating such. Again, this suggests that the ordinariates will be treated along the lines of a new ecclesial movement.

But perhaps the key section that enshrines the potentially sectarian nature of such communities comes in VIII §1, which states the following: "The Ordinary, according to the norm of law, after having heard the opinion of the Diocesan Bishop of the place, may erect, with the consent of the Holy See, personal parishes for the faithful who belong to the Ordinariate." Note the local bishop need only be asked for his opinion—the CDF in Rome has the final say over whether perceivably sectarian parishes may be established, which, in theory, means they can be imposed upon diocesan bishops in a fashion not dissimilar to, say, how some Opus Dei parishes and the like have been imposed. This suggests that episcopal collegiality and the understanding of what episcopacy means in the given setting of a diocese would be further undermined and potentially diminished. Even judicial cases need not necessarily be heard under the competency of the tribunal of the local diocese (c.f. XII).

When one looks at the actual 'Complementary Norms' issued by the CDF on November 9 (signed November 4) to accompany the Apostolic Constitution, the language at first appears to allow more say for bishops and national episcopal conferences. But one enters a chicken and egg canon law series of questions when one reads Article 2 §1, which states that "The Ordinary follows the directives of the national Episcopal Conference insofar as this is consistent with the norms contained in the Apostolic Constitution." One could interpret the latter document as already allowing more leeway than the Complementary Norms themselves, and the Apostolic Constitution certainly carries greater authority. The Norms are interpretative and simply offer mechanisms by which the Apostolic Constitution might be put into practice.

Article 3 does seem to oblige any Ordinary to "maintain close ties of communion" with the local bishop "in order to coordinate its pastoral activity" with that of the diocese,[8] but this can be interpreted in a number of ways and, as we have seen, even if the establishment of a new parish went against a bishop's wishes, the Ordinary can go over his head to Rome through the authority of the Apostolic Constitution. Indeed, he can even establish deaneries (Article 4), which require the 'approval' of Rome and the 'consent' of his own governing council[9] but merely a consultation with the national Episcopal Conference (art. 4 §3). Priests of the Ordinariate receive their faculties from their Ordinary and not the local bishop (art. 6 §3).[10] Priests and deacons of the Ordinariate can serve on diocesan presbyteral and pastoral councils (art. 8), even though the bishop has such severely limited authority over their ecclesial grouping. However, article 9 does suggest that the Ordinariate's clergy make themselves available to assist the local diocese and when doing so, they become subject to the bishop. This also works in a reciprocal fashion—when diocesan priests or religious become involved in the pastoral care of members of the Ordinariate, they are subject then to the Anglican Ordinary and not their own ordinary (be it diocesan bishop or religious superior, although they do require the permission of such to become involved in such ministry, art. 9, §2, 3).

The program of formation for the Ordinariate, while it should seek to be carried out jointly with diocesan seminarians where 'local circumstances' dictate, requires the approval of Rome, not the local bishop or episcopal conference. Here we see again why some bishops in England, Wales and the United States initially offered heavily qualified statements concerning the Apostolic Constitution. Programs of continuing formation provided by dioceses or episcopal conferences at the local level are commended to the Ordinariate (art. 10 §5).

The status of the Ordinariate's 'Governing Council' (art. 12) appears to be something that falls between an episcopal conference in miniature and a diocesan council of priests cum pastoral council (though the Ordinariate can form the latter, also, c.f. art. 13). Of course, it owes a good deal to the Anglican forms of the synodal model of governance mentioned earlier.

---

8  In the UK, so far, there is but one Ordinary, so presumably he must maintain close ties with all bishops in whose dioceses his own flock dwell.

9  Some aspects of the Anglican synodal system of government have subsequently been adopted for the Ordinariate. This is a touch ironic since those wishing to leave the Anglican church are citing many decisions and rulings of the ecclesial democratic synodal processes as key motivating factors in their decision. Many Roman Catholics will also note with some irony that the Ordinariate is obliged to establish a Pastoral Council "In order to provide for the consultation of the faithful" (XVIII §4), for, although the document here cites the *Code of Canon Law* can. 511, the notion that the laity in general should be consulted is one that has been very much out of favour in practice within the Roman Catholic Church in recent times.

10  Although the earliest ordinations in the UK were carried out by Bishops, with the Anglican Ordinary concelebrating at the mass.

One, perhaps the only, place where the requisite national episcopal conference appears to be given a major role to play (potentially) is in Article 7 §2, where the Ordinary is commanded to speak with the national conference about raising sufficient finances to take care of his clergy.

Article 5 of the Complementary Norms is where we find a perceived limitation to this new communion between erstwhile Anglicans and Roman Catholics for, as indicated, the latter may not become members of the Ordinariate, save when family circumstances appear to require it (§1). Further mixed messages are sounded by the stipulation that any Roman Catholic priest who previously became an Anglican is barred from serving as a priest in the Ordinariate (Art. 6 §2). Indeed, only former Anglicans can offer themselves for priestly formation in the Ordinariate (art. 10 §4). One of the most ambiguous sections can perhaps be found in §2 of Article 5, which speaks of laity and religious when collaborating in pastoral or charitable activities being 'subject' to the local bishop or pastor, albeit with the qualifier that such power "is exercised jointly with that of the ordinary and the Pastor of the Ordinariate."

Section III of the Apostolic Constitution appears to be issued without a hint of irony—allowing for Anglican contextualised forms of liturgy at the same time as Rome is imposing an ever-increasing normative form of liturgy across the rest of the church and showing displeasure with other forms of contextualised liturgy and worship. If the press statement accompanying the Apostolic Constitution's release was sincere in its statement that these new provisions grant "legitimate diversity in the expression of our common faith," then existing Roman Catholics have every right to ask why such diversity is not permissible elsewhere within the Roman Catholic communion as it presently stands?[11] Numerous Roman Catholics, clergy, religious, and not a few bishops in English-speaking countries have protested against the uniform imposition of a new translation of the mass and yet that translation has been railroaded through in the English-speaking church around the globe, with such concerns being totally ignored.[12] And how does all this sit with the decidedly less enthusiastic attitude towards ecumenical joint parishes between Roman Catholic and Anglicans in recent times, where more restrictive oversight is increasingly being applied, much to the dismay of those

---

11 This reminds one of Yves Congar's words, inspired by Saint Thomas, that "First of all, there can only be ecumenism if one accepts the other as other, that he also has insights, that he has something to give," 'St Thomas Aquinas and the Spirit of Ecumenism', *New Blackfriars*, Volume 55, Issue 648 (May 1974), 196–209, at 209. In one sense this latest move from Rome seeks to downplay and even negate crucial aspects of the 'otherness' of Anglicans at one and the same time as actually affirming the essential spirit of what Congar says. But the questions raised by these developments again call into doubt whether the square can genuinely be circled by this current approach from the CDF and reflected in the Apostolic Constitution. For why should there not also be otherness embraced elsewhere, such as in those other forms of inculturated worship, liturgy and interpretation and understanding of the mysteries of the faith? Or, indeed, if so many other Christian priests can indeed remain married and serve, why not also Roman Catholic priests who resigned active ministry to do so?

12 A further irony is that many of those Anglican groups seeking to join the Roman Catholic Church have relied on Roman missals and forms of prayer for some time, so maintaining a distinctively Anglican form of worship and prayer are not their main priorities.

Christians who have enjoyed the true fruits of shared communio in recent decades?

The status of former Anglican bishops presents particular ambiguities as Article 11 of the Complementary Norms details. If married they may become Ordinaries (§1) or assist the ordinary (§2) or even take part in the meetings of an Episcopal conference with the 'equivalent status' of 'a retired bishop' (§3), suddenly being made to feel not so totally null and utterly void after all,[13] much after the fashion of John Paul II's habit of gifting priestly stoles to Anglican visitors to Rome. A celibate former Anglican bishop may even ask Rome if he may "use the insignia of the Episcopal office" (§4)—hereby achieving a status still less null and void. But he can only do so if he has never been made a bishop in the Roman Catholic Church. Yes, quandaries indeed.

Thus some brief reflections upon the content of *Anglicanorum Coetibus* and the Note preceding and Norms accompanying it. Having considered what the documents have to say concerning the establishment of the Ordinariates and some of the various implications of these documents and the Ordinariates coming into being which may have been overlooked by other commentators, we now turn to consider these developments in their broader ecclesiological context.

## Discerning the Range of Implications

There are numerous implications to these norms and provisions which simply did not seem to have been taken into consideration when the ordinariates were first proposed. Indeed, given these documents were released in 2009 and the leading Anglican figures who went to Rome seeking a process by which they might 'come over' claim to have visited Rome to discuss such a move only in 2008, it could well be claimed that the regulations were drawn up and issued with undue haste.

Then there are, as we have already touched upon, profound and wide-reaching **ecumenical implications** to these developments. In particular, the ecumenically unhelpful language and tone of *Anglicanorum Coetibus*. There have been many statements, in Rome, in Britain and elsewhere, that attempt to try and square a circle by claiming that the establishment of the Ordinariates is entirely compatible with affirming and being committed to the pursuit of ecumenical unity with the Anglican Church. But such have simply failed to convince many—including at the highest levels of the Anglican Church and, privately, at the highest levels, past and present, of ecumenical representation within the Roman Catholic Church. One suspects that the resurrection of the ARICIC process and its restoration to its previous status following a lengthy period of being downplayed and downgraded on the part of Rome in some quarters, was a necessary and sensible concession wrought in part

---

13 The Ordinaries, themselves, can also attend the meetings of the national Episcopal conference with a seemingly equal voice in those deliberations.

by Rowan Williams in frank discussions with Pope Benedict XVI, and by Roman Catholic ecumenical representatives in Rome and church leaders in Britain (and perhaps elsewhere) who were astonished at the failure to consult the Pontifical Council for Christian Unity in relation to the proposed provisions for Anglican Ordinariates.

For many, in 2009, it proved somewhat difficult to accept the logic of the Note itself, and subsequent statements from the English Catholic church leadership that the commitment to ecumenism with the Anglican Church remained as important as ever. Here critics would argue that we should not forget that the present Pope, whilst Prefect of the CDF, was of the opinion that the Anglican church is not even a proper church in the full sense (it is rather an 'ecclesial community'), and he also publicly stated that Anglican ministerial orders remain 'totally null and utterly void'—a fact he appeared to suggest was a Catholic teaching taught with the charism of infallibility.[14] But aside from this, many committed ecumenists found it difficult to accept the Note as a response to a request by certain Anglicans rather than an open invitation. This, at least, posed serious threats to decades of good work between Anglicans and Roman Catholics at both the official and additional levels that had so dramatically improved relations between these Christians and genuinely fostered *koinonia*.[15]

For many ecumenists, the evidence appeared to suggest that more recent developments constituted a going back on both the spirit and letter of Vatican II, and the ecumenical openness and progress that the Council and its era

---

14 A point which, when expressed in 1998, was a personal opinion rather than an 'official' teaching. Papal Bulls and Encyclicals are not—in the main—ways of exercising teaching with the charism of infallibility, thus the understanding of Anglican orders in Leo XIII's Bull, *Apostolicae Curae*, of 1896 was presumed by many to be open to further debate, not least of all due to changing circumstances such as subsequent harmonious relations between Anglicans and the Old Catholic church. But note the conundrum—then Cardinal Ratzinger's opinion was not a teaching offered with the charism of infallibility—even on his own admission. Therefore the status of teachings declared to be 'definitive' via a statement of non-definitive status is logically open to scrutiny and can be the subject of legitimate 'dissent'.

15 Although statements issued by Pope Benedict on his subsequent visit to Britain in September 2010, such as his speech at Oscott College on September 19, further affirmed the commitment to the seeking of ecumenical unity with Anglicans, this was, of course, very much after the fact of the release of the documents announcing the establishment of the Ordinariate and would no doubt have had input from and approval by Roman Catholic ecumenists, including those working in Britain. Given the protocol on such occasions and visits, it is likely some Anglicans had sight of the text before it was read, also. At Oscott, Pope Benedict reminded the English and Welsh Catholic bishops how he had asked them to respond 'generously' to the proposed Ordinariate in their country when they visited Rome in February, 2010. He went on to say, "This should be seen as a prophetic gesture that can contribute positively to the developing relations between Anglicans and Catholics. It helps us to set our sights on the ultimate goal of all ecumenical activity: the restoration of full ecclesial communion," full text available at http://www.thepapalvisit.org.uk/Replay-the-Visit/Speeches/Speeches-19-September/Pope-Benedict-s-Address-at-Oscott-College (accessed June 20, 2011). The sentiment concerning the link between the establishment of the Ordinariate and full unity between Catholics and Anglicans is underlined further still by the official commentary on the establishment of the Ordinariate offered by the English and Welsh Bishops Conference through their website. There they cite these words from Benedict and follow them with the statement, "In this way, the establishment of the Ordinariate is clearly intended to serve the wider and unchanging aim of the full visible unity between the Catholic Church and the members of the Anglican Communion" (http://www.catholic-ew.org.uk/Catholic-Church/Ordinariate/Background-Information, accessed May 24, 2011).

helped generate in many ways. Such might also be interpreted as part of those wider ecclesial trends we have discussed.[16] This requires a little further explanation. The concern for ecumenists is that language of both the Note and *Anglicanorum Coetibus*, itself, are decidedly of the flavour of the 'return to the true church' understanding of 'ecumenism' that many had hoped was banished by Vatican II and subsequent bi-lateral and multi-lateral efforts.

There are implications for the ecclesial being, the lives of Christian communities at the levels of the Anglican communion itself and the Roman Catholic Church worldwide. Then there are the implications for the churches at a national level where Ordinariates will be established, both in terms of the Anglican national churches and the Roman Catholic Church in those countries. This is a particularly acute issue in the United Kingdom where Roman Catholics are a small yet nonetheless prominent minority religious grouping. Then there are the implications for ecclesial life at the diocesan and deanery levels and then, crucially, at the parish level (and even further, possibly within particular families).

Not least of all the opening of the latter document refers to receiving Anglicans 'into full Catholic communion'. This could only have been a very carefully chosen phrase, pregnant as it is with decidedly partial ecclesiological undertones and with deep ecumenical implications. So many Anglicans consider themselves and profess each Sunday their existing belief in the Catholic church. Furthermore, there did not at the time appear to be any sensitivity or forethought given to the very real danger that the provisions *Anglicanorum Coetibus* set in place might actually lead to some harm coming to the very unity of the church it lauds. This is because, at all levels, the establishment of the Ordinariate offers a further mechanism by which literally sectarian 'churches' within the local church can flourish to a great extent aside from the life, norms and governance of that local church. This mirrored the developments concerning the naming of Opus Dei as a 'personal prelature' of the Pope himself, under Pope John Paul II. Although section I§1 of *Anglicanorum Coetibus* speaks of consultation with the relevant episcopal conference where an Ordinariate is to be founded, it was nonetheless obvious and was subsequently confirmed that this document was prepared and released without any such consultation. This continues a trend of downplaying the authority and significance of national Episcopal conferences reflected throughout much of the theology of Joseph Ratzinger and his public pronouncements whilst Prefect of the CDF.

---

16 Critics believe that a form of 'restorationism' is linked to this agenda. In *The Ratzinger Report*, Ratzinger clarifies how he understands the term 'restoration' to mean not so much a turning back but rather, true to its semantic roots, 'a recovery of values within a new totality', 38, n.5. He adds, "But if by restoration we understand the search for a new balance after all the exaggerations of an indiscriminate opening to the world, after the overly positive interpretations of an agnostic and atheistic world, well, then a restoration understood in this sense (a newly found balance of orientations and values within the Catholic totality) is altogether desirable and, for that matter, is already in operation in the Church. In this sense it can be said that the first phase after Vatican II has come to a close," *ibid.*, 37–38.

These developments reflect the preferment for 'new ecclesial movement', now linked closely to the agenda for the 'new evangelization' that has been central to the priorities of Rome for some time in one form or another. Various movements in the church are given great latitude and independence from the local diocesan bishops, largely because they appear to follow an ecclesial agenda and ecclesiological vision that resonates with that most prominent in Rome in recent decades. These other movements have frequently been accused of adopting practices and stances that are separatist, elitist and indeed ecclesially divisive, as well as being secretive.

If the ordinariates are not being envisioned to develop in the same fashion as these other new ecclesial movements, further question here concerns the necessity of the ordinariates at all, for any individual Anglican could always have become Roman Catholic. What happens now is not so much that entire congregations of Anglicans might come over to Rome collectively, although such is likely to continue to happen in some cases, but rather there will be 'a people set apart' by various circumstances and practices, not to say attitudes, existing alongside Roman Catholics in their own parishes, dioceses and nations. Guidelines issued in England and Wales state that any member of the Ordinariate can worship in any Roman Catholic parish alongside other Roman Catholics. The opposite is also the case—Roman Catholics who are not members of the Ordinariate can also worship at the services of the latter. But one vital difference is noted here: existing Roman Catholics cannot become members of the Ordinariate—not even if they were once Anglicans.[17]

Note that the 'Ordinary' who will lead this movement in a given place will, in many respects, have equivalent status to (and indeed can even be) a bishop. But, unlike diocesan bishops who exercise 'immediate' authority pertaining to the territory of a diocese, as canon law states, the reach of the authority of the Anglican Ordinary will be through authority that is 'personal' to the Ordinariate and so can move beyond and across the boundaries of existing parishes, deaneries and dioceses. And while the diocesan bishop exercises his 'power' in his own name, the Anglican Ordinary will do so vicariously on behalf of the Pope.

There is an irony in all this. The Church of England, and essentially Anglicanism with it, was borne out of various political intrigues of the sixteenth century and fueled by zeal for religious reform by a number within its ranks. It was a church condemned for wishing to 'go its own way' first in terms of governance and later in terms of worship, theology, ministry etc. It will now see former Anglicans breaking with the central communion and authority of Anglicanism on the one hand, and largely bypassing the authority of local Roman Catholic bishops and national episcopal conferences on the other, and being assisted in all this by the Bishop of Rome and the successor to the Holy Office of the Inquisition.

---

17 C.f. Bill Tammeus, 'US Episcopalians await Catholic Welcome' in *National Catholic Reporter* (May 23, 2011), http://ncronline.org/news/us-episcopalians-await-catholic-welcome (accessed May 23, 2011).

Legitimate concerns have been voiced about whether such developments might not actually harm the communio that forms so prominent a feature of official Catholic ecclesiology in recent times, and is even more pronounced in the theological writings of Joseph Ratzinger across decades, and which features as an important concept in the text of *Anglicanorum Coetibus* from itself. For the bonds of unity fostered through this document primarily seem to be between select groups of Anglicans who hold particularly reactionary ecclesiological views and Rome, as opposed to between Anglicans and Roman Catholics at the parish, local community, deanery, diocesan and national levels.

The announcement of the Apostolic Constitution and Complementary Norms on the feast of St. Charles Borromeo also offer some rich symbolism, for the much revered pious saint was something of a fixer for his uncle, Pope Pius IV, helping secure support for the Pope's priorities at the Council of Trent and then later, as bishop and cardinal, helping to implement the Tridentine reforms. Charles had notable connections with English Roman Catholicism, helping to support the English College at Douai and hosting two of the future English martyrs in Edmund Campion and Ralph Sherwin. An amazing, full and all too short life. But is this bastion of Tridentine reform and particularly of its application against the then still-in-formation Church of England the most ecumenically appropriate saint on whose feast to release these documents, if the sincere commitment to unity with Anglicans is genuinely still held?

The Press Release that accompanied the Constitution's release certainly seemed accurate in its statement that the Constitution "opens a new avenue for the promotion of Christian unity;" but sadly it appears to be one that works against other, more wide-ranging paths towards greater harmony between these two churches. As early as 2009, meetings of ecumenical groups have had their agendas taken over by the expression of concerns by non-Roman Catholics that these developments signal the advent of a new approval of proselytising as the 'future' of the path to Christian 'unity'.

## Wider Ecclesiological Implications

We turn to examine but a few of the wider ecclesiological implications, i.e., what the provisions for these Ordinariates imply and indeed make concrete in terms of the self-understanding of the church held by Anglicans making such a journey 'across the Tiber' and by the Roman Catholic authorities. For example, one reads at the very beginning of *Anglicanorum Coetibus* statements with profound ecclesiological significance. The Holy Spirit is credited with moving certain Anglicans to seek such a pathway, just as the Holy Spirit (echoing *Lumen gentium* 13 and Acts 2:42) is "the principle of unity, which establishes the Church as a communion." Of course, few Christians would disagree in relation to the latter, but the former statement is simply an interpretation attributing an authority and rectitude to the motivations and therefore actions of a group of individuals that others might contest. And such contestation need not cast any aspersions upon the sincerity of the intentions of any individual Anglican, it simply points out that it is wiser to speak with less certitude about where and when and how the Spirit moves. We know from church history that, all too often, many believe or claim to be acting under the impulses of the Spirit when the evidence might suggest that the Spirit is simultaneously moving the church and many within it in a significantly different direction.

This tone and style in the document (which has been replicated in parts of the official statements in places such as Britain in the lead up and aftermath of the first Anglicans joining the Ordinariate) does, however, mirror the tone, style and form of numerous other documents that have issued from Rome in recent decades whereby the dividing line between doctrinal statements and their requisite authority and the mere interpretation of ecclesial attitudes and actions become significantly blurred. To reiterate, church leaders, including popes, have often suggested that actions and intentions have been the will of God or the stirrings of the Spirit when the evidence either at the time or subsequently has cast doubt or indeed disproved such claims. Church councils and subsequent popes and church leaders have been adept at ensuring that such erroneous views can be rectified. One notable example, of course, concerns the absolutist interpretation and affirmation of the *dictum extra ecclesiam nulla salus*.[18] What appears missing from this process is enough time and depth of engagement by all significant parties concerned in the due processes of ecumenical deliberation and ecclesial discernment.

A further ecclesiological concern raised by *Anglicanorum Coetibus* is the understanding of the church exhibited at the outset of that document itself. In a passage where we read that "The Church, however, analogous to the mystery of the incarnate Word, is not only an invisible spiritual communion, but it is also visible," what follows requires significant ecclesiological attention. Although the document cites selectively from and references *Lumen gentium*, we see another familiar practice with many Roman documents in recent times, whereby what is being offered is an interpretation of what *Lumen gentium* says and means and an interpretation that would be contested by many Roman Catholics.[19]

The problematic pattern referred to here is the manner in which certain church teaching documents, most notably from Vatican II, are being reinterpreted and have certain passages taken out of context and juxtaposed with later and, some would say, differing and even divergent ecclesiological

---

18  Here c.f., for example, Charles E. Curran (ed.), *Change in Official Catholic Moral Teachings, Readings in Moral Theology* vol. 13 (New York, Paulist Press, 2003).

19  Other well-known examples where such a practice is followed include *Dominus Iesus* (2000) and 'Note on the Expression "Sister Churches"' (2007). Here c.f. Gerard Mannion, 'Roman Catholicism and its Religious "Others": Contemporary Challenges' in Gerard Mannion (ed.), *Church and Religious Other: Essays on Truth, Unity and Diversity* (London and New York: T&T Clark, 2008), 126–153.

perspectives in order to try and communicate continuity between the Second Vatican Council and the ecclesiology currently preferred in authoritative Roman circles and elsewhere. What takes place in *Anglicanorum Coetibus* could be interpreted as moving away from the more ecumenically open intentions of *Lumen gentium* and the Council in general.

So, following the statement of the unity between the invisible and visible church, (again citing *Lumen gentium* §8), *Anglicanorum Coetibus* states the following, "The communion of the baptized in the teaching of the Apostles and in the breaking of the Eucharistic bread is visibly manifested in the bonds of the profession of the faith in its entirety, of the celebration of all the sacraments instituted by Christ, and of the governance of the College of Bishops united with its head, the Roman Pontiff." At this point, in its footnote the Constitution cites—without explication—an array of diverse ecclesial documents.[20]

Here, then, *Lumen gentium's* words are juxtaposed with what is essentially a blueprint 'official' ecclesiology that repeats those elements said in recent church documents to be necessary in order for a church to be considered authentic.[21] Indeed here it appears to go further still and add to these criteria the governance of the Pope himself and the College of bishops. The message that could be taken away from these statements is that Anglicans who are seeking to become Roman Catholics are affirming that their own church is deficient in relation to a number of significant and vital ecclesial and ecclesiological aspects. In the very least, the language and tone of the document here and in other places are ecumenically unhelpful.

The Council sought to affirm and acknowledge that the church is more than the Roman Catholic Church, and the small passage that has generated so much discussion subsequently, viz., the 'subsistit in' passage of *Lumen gentium* §8, by and large was intended to underscore this positive and inclusive ecclesiological shift. But in more recent decades the interpretation of that passage and indeed of *Lumen gentium* and the council more generally have been reassessed and attempts have been made to offer more ecumenically restrictive interpretations. The subsistit in passage is actually cited in *Anglicanorum Coetibus* at this very point.

The issue which ecumenically minded ecclesiologists would raise here is that a passage the Council fathers intended to be a highly significant statement of ecumenical openness has been elsewhere and now again appears to be, in *Anglicanorum Coetibus*, employed and interpreted in a fashion that accentuates the superiority of the Roman Catholic Church vis-à-vis other churches or 'ecclesial communions' (to cite the preferred terminology in church documents from recent times that deny that some churches are

---

20  Including the *Code of Canon Law*, can. 205, *Lumen gentium* §§13, 14, 21, 22; *Unitatis redintegratio* §§2, 3, 4, 15, 20; the decree *Christus Dominus*, §4 and the decree *Ad gentes* §22.

21  Again, c.f. *Dominus Iesus* (2000) and 'Note on the Expression "Sister Churches"' (2007).

actually proper churches at all). This further echoes the older ecclesiological identification between the Church of Christ and the Roman Catholic Church.

Here, *Anglicanorum Coetibus* might even be deemed to imply a return to a fundamental ecclesiology more resonant with Pius XII's *Mystici Corporis Christi*, as, along with its echoing of the normative ecclesiological perspective of *Communionis notio* to which *Anglicanorum Coetibus* makes reference, there is a danger here that what is being stated—whether it is actually meant to be communicated or not—is that the Roman Catholic institutional church is once again to be deemed as equivalent to the Church itself, with the requisite implications of such a perception to the status of other churches. Ecclesiologically and ecumenically, the tone and language are problematic. Dialogical sensitivities should at least have warranted that unambiguously positive language in ecumenical terms would have been preferable.

## A (Strange) Sort of Homecoming?

Taking all of the foregoing into account for today's church, one of the key questions must be: what is it that an Anglican might hope to gain—in the twenty-first century—by going 'over' to Rome? At the moment some might argue that it seems the primary gain is simply an encouragement to maintain beliefs and practices which run contrary to not simply the moral consciousness of our present-day communities, but also the Christian faith itself which has done so much to shape and inform that moral consciousness.

Answers to this question may have been very different at various stages of history in the story of Anglicanism. There may have been periods when Anglicans in particular contexts might well have gained something personally or communally positive in making such a move, or they may have been following their conscience in taking such a path. There have been and may continue to be circumstances where familial or geographical circumstances or even fear or, indeed, persecution might have necessitated the formalising of a relationship with the Roman Catholic Church.

But none of these possible reasons seem to be applicable today with regard to those Anglicans in question here. Talk of Anglicans 'coming home', whether from Anglicans themselves or from Roman Catholics, appears to be something of a category mistake in the twenty-first century, in the wake of the great efforts taken towards ecumenical progress between these churches in the twentieth century. Indeed, unless one has a very crude and historically uninformed understanding of the coming into being of the churches that emerged out of the period of European reformations and the subsequent development of those churches and their fluctuating relationship with the Roman Catholic communion, then this talk of 'coming home' is rather like somebody in a very large single-story residence donning their overcoat and announcing they are 'off home' only to move from the parlour to the dining room. For ecclesial and existential logic suggests that their dwelling place is the household of God, and the particular house in question here is the Christian church itself. The Church of Christ is the home of Anglicans. They are already at their destination. No taxi required. Therefore talk of conversion from Canterbury to Rome is another category mistake for, as Roman Catholic teaching makes clear, one's conversion, one's metanoia is to Christ and his entire body, which is neither to be identified with nor exhausted by the Roman Catholic Church itself. This is the true meaning behind *Lumen gentium*[22] (as opposed to the impression readers might take away from the third paragraph of *Anglicanorum Coetibus* which appears to be citing *Lumen gentium*.[23]

There may well be genuine 'translations' for an individual and even sometimes groups of people and communities to new situations where they feel they are more existentially able to flourish in another church. The question is still open for debate whether it is really possible for a Christian to 'convert' out of one ecclesial-existential mode of being into another so as to nullify wholly and permanently their previous mode of being. And much debated it is.

None of this is to pretend serious issues and divisions do not still exist between the Roman Catholic and Anglican churches. Doctrinal, liturgical, ecclesiological, practical and moral, not to mention hermeneutical differences, all remain, although the same can be said to be the case with regard to each Christian denomination. Indeed, according to the 'trans-denominational reformation' theory, such divisions are witnessed increasingly within communions *ad intra*, thereby potentially making the differences across the Roman Catholic/Anglican divide less of a reason to maintain divisions or, indeed, to 'move' from one church to another. For neither certitude nor universal agreement on contentious issues will be gained by such a move.

If the mutual excommunications between the Orthodox churches and Roman Catholicism as a source of division can be overcome, then the time has come to revisit openly and honestly the historical backdrop to Anglican-Roman Catholic relations. In particular, Henry VIII's various personal and political peccadillos, and the expedient rejection of papal authority they necessitated, sparked the subsequent ebb and flow in the life of the English church and beyond that followed. This should not be visited upon Anglicans in perpetuity. In other words, we must ask, in the twenty-first century, whether there are any genuinely insurmountable stumbling blocks remaining on the path towards closer unity.

Before such debates are explored in full, one might suggest that any 'jumping ship' must remain premature, at the very least. In the meantime, *Anglicanorum Coetibus* and its accompanying norms and Note may well be deemed to remain ecumenically unhelpful and even a setback to the cause of ecumenism further still because of implied further negative

---

22 C.f., e.g., *Lumen gentium*, §8, 10. Ironically, both these sections of the Vatican II Dogmatic Constitution on the Church are mentioned in footnotes by *Anglicanorum Coetibus* itself.

23 *Lumen gentium* made clear the church of Christ is *not* identical with and confined to the Roman Catholic Church alone.

qualitative judgments about Anglicanism per se and its perceived 'deficiencies'. Furthermore, these documents have been already perceived as a reassertion of the proselytising 'return to Rome, the one true church' agenda by many protestants and Anglicans alike. The tone, manner of composition, and nature and date of release of official church documents are often, in many ways, also theological and particularly ecclesiological statements in and of themselves. It was with no irony that many people noted how the Canadian Anglicans and Catholics affirmed their joint commitment for working towards greater unity on the very day the CDF 'Note' was released, and also that in England, itself, birthplace of Anglicanism, fruitful conversations about renewed efforts towards ecumenical dialogue were equally shaken by their release.

But if Anglican-Roman Catholic dialogues today are to remain sincere, if the ecumenical efforts are to remain genuine and not simply versions of the growing trend in risk-free politeness that can pass for ecumenism and interfaith dialogue, then might it rather be the duty of Anglicans, even those with concerns about their own church at present, to stay where they ecclesially are and work for the unity Christ prayed for. And this would be unity, first, amongst Anglicans themselves, and second between Anglicans and other Christians, including Roman Catholics. Indeed, there needs to be a further series of extensive debates about what such unity might entail and indeed about the very concept itself.

But perhaps the most decisive argument against anyone making the journey 'over to Rome' is that there are just as many divisions within the Roman Catholic Church, including many relating to the same issues as those which bitterly divide Anglicans at present. Anglicans making such a journey would simply be entering a room where the same arguments are taking place, perhaps with different insults being traded, perhaps with those arguments at different stages—some at much earlier stages, but many at much more advanced stages.

Anglicans heading towards Rome must also desist themselves of any notion that Roman Catholicism is uniform in other ways, whether doctrinal, liturgical, theological, structural, ministerial or otherwise. They must especially resist any assumption that they would enter into a world of Evelyn Waugh or John Henry Newman—for there are appallingly lifeless forms of worship and parish life in the Roman Catholic Church, too. And if structural, ministerial or liturgical differences are what really motivate some Anglicans to make such a move, why can they not stay where they are and seek to influence debates within and perhaps even effect such changes within their own local, diocesan, national or regional churches?

And if the motivation is the oft-cited question of authority, then, once again, history and Roman Catholic teaching itself can both illustrate that their perspective here might be misinformed or too narrow. And this is not to mention the intricate debates surrounding questions of authority and the broader sense of magisterium itself currently preoccupying so many within the Roman Catholic church.[24]

Indeed, these developments surrounding the Ordinariate could, themselves, be interpreted as symptomatic of a wider, even systemic, malaise in the Roman Catholic Church with regard to magisterium. For it could be argued that the CDF, in taking these initiatives, has once again exceeded its genuine authority and usurped that magisterium proper to other parts of the church,[25] not least of all the college of Bishops, the (Roman Catholic) episcopal conferences in countries where there are significant numbers of Anglicans, the Pontifical Council for Christian Unity and, certainly not least of all, the non-ordained Roman Catholic faithful and indeed clergy and religious in those countries affected by the provisions introduced.

Add to this the ecumenical duty to involve significant elements of Anglican magisterium in this process—largely the mirror image or analogous elements of those mentioned above—but certainly, for example, the Archbishops of Canterbury (and, indeed, Westminster) should have been consulted from the outset, along with those involved in the earlier phases of ARCIC and related discussion bodies.

Finally, and again not least, such developments have ignored and bypassed the authority and *sensus fidelium* of Anglican non-ordained faithful and clergy and religious in differing countries most likely to be affected by the new provisions. Roman Catholic and Anglican theologians could have contributed to this discussion, along with those from other churches, about the impact this would have on wider ecumenical efforts. Perhaps the establishment of Ordinariates might have formed a legitimate topic of discussion for the recently re-convened ARCIC meetings. All of these are elements of magisterium that should have been involved in deliberations over such provisions long before any decision was reached, let alone the release of an Apostolic Constitution and accompanying Norms.

Not even a Pope, and certainly not a curial department such as the CDF, is at liberty to try and persuade the faithful that black is white or vice-versa. A grey area enters into the fray when what were previously personal theological opinions—be they on the part of curial officials or those in higher office, including popes—become 'official' church teaching and policy. Ecumenical discussions should have taken place concerning what the actual basis and authoritative status of the opinions behind *Anglicanorum Coetibus* and the

---

24 Here c.f. Gerard Mannion, 'Defending the Faith': The Changing Landscape of Church Teaching Authority and Catholic Theology—1978-2005', in Gerard Mannion (ed.), *The Vision of John Paul II: Assessing His Thought and Influence* (Collegeville, MN, Liturgical Press, 2008), 78-106; and Gerard Mannion, 'A Teaching Church that Learns? Discerning Authentic Teaching for Our Times', in *The Crisis of Authority in Catholic Modernity*, eds. Michael J. Lacey and Francis Oakley (Oxford and New York, Oxford University Press, March 2011), 161-191. A forthcoming monograph treatment of these questions will be published in 2012: *A Teaching Church That Learns*, Collegeville, MN., Liturgical Press.

25 C.f. an analogous discussion in relation to *Dominus Iesus* in 2000, Thomas Rausch, "Has the Congregation for the Doctrine of the Faith Exceeded its Authority?" *Theological Studies* 62:4 (2001), 802-810.

ecclesial transformations it has set in motion actually were. It will serve the ecumenical cause well if they actually now do take place.

## Some Tentative Conclusions: The Ecumenical Responsibilities of Contemporary Anglicans and Roman Catholics

Obviously, it is not for a Roman Catholic to seek to pass judgement on the current disagreements within Anglicanism—partly out of ecclesial and ecumenical courtesy and etiquette, and partly because all Roman Catholics are so blinded by the beam of intra-ecclesial divisions in their own eyes. But here the words of an esteemed Anglican ecclesiologist are highly pertinent. Paul Avis, mindful of the serious problems besetting the whole world of our times, reminds us all that,

> The New Testament is gripped by the urgency of spreading the gospel of Christ, hastening the coming of God's kingdom and glorifying God in all that we do in our personal lives and in the common life of the church. Anglicans should have a bad conscience about squandering energy on internal squabbles while God yearns to redeem the world. People looking on, sometimes wistfully, from the sidelines draw their own conclusions about the relevance of the gospel.[26]

Avis does not mean to trivialise the issues over which Anglicans are divided—quite the opposite, as his wider essay clearly demonstrates. It is the pettiness that clouds conversations over these issues within his church that he finds objectionable.

There are many debates about the perceived 'myth' of the Anglican Communion, if the latter is understood in terms of being analogous to, say, Roman Catholicism in form, structure and polity, etc.[27] But Anglicans have traditional gifts that can help all Christians overcome divisions, and so perhaps now is the time to accentuate the value of those gifts towards affirming truly inculturated forms of Anglicanism wherever Anglicans strive to live out the Gospel today.

But in terms of the broader ecclesial scene I have touched upon here, the 'trans-denominational' reformation certainly gives all Christians much cause for concern in many respects and the painful internecine struggles of Anglicanism, which are perhaps acutely mirrored especially in Canada and the United States, are vivid illustrations of both how and why this is so. In terms of the debates about mission and proclamation, I think Christians in all churches today need to have the courage to stand firm and not return to the path towards competition, conflict and withdrawal from their societies

---

26 Avis, 'Anglican Ecclesiology', 202–203.
27 C.f. the essays by Mark Chapman and George Pattison, in Gerard Mannion (ed.), *Church and Religious Other* (London and New York, T & T Clark/Continuum, 2008).

and the wider world that lies in the perception of mission as conversion. Rather we might seek to renew the commitment to understanding dialogue as being a rich form of proclamation—and indeed we can all come to understand this even in intra-ecclesial terms. Ecumenism applies as much within one's church as without—by definition it is a concept with universal application. Perhaps, in these times, dialogue with the ecclesial others in our own churches is one of the most important forms of witness to the Gospel in which we can engage.

However, given the various developments we have considered here, perhaps one outcome of these shifting ecclesial and ecclesiological sands might actually be—in the long term—greater substantial progress towards more visible and genuine elements of unity. I mean unity here not à la the sense of a 'lifeboat to Rome', or in the sense used by the CDF 'Note' and Norms on personal Anglican Ordinariates and *Anglicanorum Coetibus* itself, which appear, for many, to be too reminiscent of an ecumenical vision being one of return to the 'true' sheepfold. Rather I mean that as more and more Christians across the differing denominations come to realise and, crucially, appreciate, that what they share in common, what unites them, *where*, to use Roger Haight's phrase, 'they dwell in common',[28] then the more likely they will come to appreciate that such are infinitely more important than what divides them. Strange ecclesial bedfellows can be found all over the church in these times. Is this a mischievous Holy Spirit at work in the service of greater ecumenical unity?

If perfect ecclesial unity, or indeed uniformity, ever existed in the church, then the concept of *koinonia* or communion would, in many ways, have been superfluous.[29] As well as affirming plurality and unity in diversity, the purpose of such a concept is really to help us to periodically re-imagine our multiple belongings and our ways and means of relationality for differing times and contexts.

Indeed, in many ways, the term unity, itself, can sometimes prove a stumbling block for what is often perceived by the world as 'uniformity' and the removal of difference and local custom. Those explorations into the concept and real entailments of what is meant when we speak of unity need to begin soon and in as fully and inclusive manner as necessary. Until if or when the term unity can be re-envisioned and more helpfully clarified, the notion of 'partial communion' might be preferable, helpful and more facilitative of what is really intended by the employment of the term unity by so many committed ecumenists.[30]

For such ecclesial unity may necessarily take the form of partial

---

28 Roger Haight, *Ecclesial Existence*, vol. 3 of *Comparative Ecclesiology* (New York and London, Continuum), 2008.

29 At least understood in its 'horizontal' forms, aside from those 'vertical' aspects pertaining to communion with God's own very triune self.

30 This concept receives a nuanced and ecumenically creative treatment in Haight, *Ecclesial Existence* (New York and London, Continuum, 2008).

communion in the future, but in many ways this is what most Christians have enjoyed for much of the history of the church. Partial communion does not mean a qualitative decrease in mutuality and interdependence. Rather it can be the utmost exercise of ecclesial responsibility. Given that there is no such thing as un-inculturated Christian being, no such thing as an acontex-tualised church, how could it be otherwise? Anglicans have illustrated and appreciated this for most of the existence of the more specifically identifi-able inculturated and contextualised forms of being church that claim the Anglican identity. These are not the times to forget the virtues of being a truly broad church. Catholicity, then, is understood here in qualitative terms— both synchronically and diachronically.

Speaking as a Roman Catholic, I offer some penultimate words from a wise old priest whose words might convince us that neither 'jumping ship' nor responding 'generously' to sectarian advances is really the duty of Christians today, rather we are called to genuine engagement and dialogue in order to appreciate better that dwelling place that all who follow Christ share in common,

> . . . we have to force each other mutually to be and to become as Christian as possible, and to understand what is really radical about the Christian message a little better. Even in its divisions Christianity today exists in a historical, social, cultural and spiritual situation which obliges all of these separated Christians to ask themselves how they do justice to the future which is pressing upon us. And where the theolo-gies of the different churches are making an effort really to answer the questions which a non-Christian age is posing to Christianity, there will always be the best chance that this new theology being done by people who belong to different churches will slowly develop a theological unity from out of the questions being proposed to all of them in common. This unity will then move beyond many of the controversial theological problems which at the moment are insoluble, and will render them to a certain extent otiose.[31]

In the twenty-first century, the kindly light might best be understood as seeking to provide not a guide along the path of movement from one church to another, even if that be to the Anglican's 'ever-beloved sister', as Paul VI called the Anglican church, but rather to offer the greater illumination of the place wherein they are already dwelling. With greater light and warmth in the room, perhaps people need be less fearful and uncomfortable and may be able actually to see, communicate with, understand and perhaps even enjoy joyous relations with all those with whom they share their part of this dwelling place.

---

31  Karl Rahner, *Foundation of Christian Faith* (New York, Crossroad, 1994), 369.

# AFTERWORD

*Martyn Percy*

> Biologically, life is not maintenance or restoration of equilibrium, but is essentially the maintenance of dis-equilibrium, as the doctrine of open systems reveals. Reaching equilibrium means death and decay.
>
> —Bruce Reed, *The Dynamics of Religion*, 1978

For many faiths, balance is merely finding the midpoint between liberalism and conservatism, or perhaps traditionalist and progressive. Faiths of all kinds strive to find a way of being, living, and moving forward that keep together a tense synthesis of values, priorities, symbols, and beliefs. Anglicanism is not unique in this regard. Indeed, it is in some respects a fairly typical expression of faith in the modern world, trying to mediate between past and present, or perhaps dissenters and conformists. As a faith, it is a fusion of tensions; and as such, it often expresses itself best not in uniformity, but a unity that is rooted in discussion, debate, and sometimes disagreement.

The point of balance, for Anglicans, is often elusive. It does not lie in a static, compromised middle ground, or in some (fondly imagined?) "broad church" of yesteryear. The point of balance, for Anglicans, lies in the mutual and respectful comprehension of otherness. As such, the broad middle ground of Anglicanism is often, perhaps surprisingly, the front line or cutting edge; it is the radical, difficult place to be. It is arguably easy to belong to one of the many enclaves or tribal proclivities that make up the rich diversity of Anglican life. Being a conservative evangelical or conservative Catholic delivers a worldview replete with real clarity on allies and enemies. But to hold on to and occupy a place of mediation that retains the poise and composure of the whole body—as many in positions of oversight, whether ecclesial or governmental—is never easy. Maintaining balance is, of course, not an end in itself. It is, rather, that method and ethos that enables all of the life forces of the body—in their intracompetiveness and complementarity—to empower and shape the whole body. The point of balance is that it enables diversity; it permits opposites to contribute, dialogue, debate, disagree, and unite—but in a tense range of spectra. It moves a body from shallow uniformity to a distractive and rich unity. It enables different weights to coexist in tension. Crucially, the point of balance is often *not* the midpoint, but rather the point at which all the different weights can be held and suspended to perform a deeper task.

It is something of a caricature of Anglicanism to describe it in "middling terms." Anglican polity as neither hot nor cold: just warm. The classic *via media*; Laodicean, tepid—and proud of it. Anglicanism is born of England, and like its climate, it is often a temperate polity; cloudy, occasional sunny spells and the odd shower—but no extremes. "Redeemed mildness" is another way of expressing it, perhaps. But the English like to discuss the weather, most which is akin to our polity. We complain if it is too hot . . . and too cold. Goldilocks has it right—we look for the warm middle. Anglicans are not alone in this. Even Wesley, as a good Anglican, only had his heart "strangely warmed"—not hot, then. Indeed, Methodists often celebrate their temperateness.

But what happens in congregations and denominations when things get a bit too heated? Some churches, of course, like intensity and heat; it is a sign of vibrant life and feisty faith. But others who are of a more temperate hue find this disturbing; heated exchanges, anger, and passions seem to dismay more than they comfort. Anglicanism is a *via media*—what Archbishop Robert Runcie once described as "passionate coolness." This is a typically Anglican phrase—the framing of ecclesial identity within an apparent paradox. But you could say that what currently afflicts Anglicanism is not this or that issue—but the heat and intensity that often accompany the debates— because Anglicans are used to temperate, cool debates. We don't tend to do anger well; we don't cope well with excess. So the churches that are used to heat both climatologically and theologically can conflict with the more traditionally temperate culture. And when heat meets coolness, a storm can brew.

The worldwide Anglican Communion contains a great many varieties of tensions. On the surface, some of the most manifest difficulties appear to be centred on issues such as sexuality, gender, the right use of the Bible, and the appropriate interpretation of Scripture. It is therefore possible to narrate the schismatic tendencies in Anglicanism with reference to authority, theology, and ecclesial power. But on its own, as a thesis, this is clearly inadequate, as such tensions have existed within Anglicanism from the outset. There has not been a single century in which Anglicanism has not wrestled with its identity; it is by nature a polity that draws on a variety of competing theological traditions. Its very appeal lies in its own distinctive hybridity. Indeed, hybridity is an important key in understanding the wisdom of God—in Christ, his incarnate son—who chooses to work through miscibility rather than purity. Anglicans are born of compromise; it is where we found and find God.

Indeed, we can go further here, and suggest that all Christian history, generally, is a history of progression through *tense meetings*. The great councils of Nicea and Chalcedon, or the debates at Worms, the Reformations in Europe, right the way through to the First and Second Vatican Councils, are gatherings of opposites. These are places where ideas clash, are discerned and distilled, before slowly forming into a rich harmony infused with tension and agreement. As any parish priest knows, it is no different in the local church. Christians work through differences to find common ground. Debates, dissention, and disagreement are never indicators of denominations in their early death-throes. These dynamics are, rather, as Bruce Reed suggests, signs of life that point to vitality. The point of balance, then, is the space and place where a sufficient degree of unity is achieved to enable the body to regain the poise it needs to hold its diversities together. Balance is born of wisdom and maturity. Balance is not a political position that simply acts to sedate endless vacillation. Rather, it is the place that allows competitive and tense life forces in the body to continue contributing to the total well-being of that body, and to our wider social polity.

Balance, then, is something that enables unity, but does not confuse it with uniformity. Yeats' famous poem mourned that "things fall apart—the centre cannot hold." But the centre was always contested, not settled. So what is to be done? No single solution presents itself. Recognising that there are cultural factors in shaping and individuating churches is important. Valuing diversity alongside unity will always be vital. And praying fervently with Jesus "that we may all be one" will also be crucial—although perhaps muttering in the same breath: "but thank God we are all different." As this collection of essays suggests, we as Anglicans should perhaps celebrate our diversity a little more. It is evidence of strength, not weakness.

But does that mean anything goes, as long as it can be balanced? Clearly not. Affirming diversity need not be a "counsel of despair." Far from it. There *is* a homogenous faith polity that Anglicans can identify and celebrate. But it is important to understand the ecclesial nature of that body. The first Lambeth Conference gathered because of disunity, not unity. In 1867, as now, a number of bishops refused to come. But it was not a disaster. Conflict is not a bad thing in itself; it can be creative and point to maturity in polity that is the envy of narrower ecclesiological frames of reference. Conflict can challenge commitment and breathe life into the connections that configure communion. Church is, after all, a long-term community composed out of committed relationships. It is not a short-term project or relationship that depends on agreement in the present; let alone an immediacy of rapport. In Communion—just like a good marriage—Anglicans work *through* conflict and difficulty; our faithfulness to God and one another sees to it that we find enrichment rather than weakness in our apparent tiffs and tantrums.

That said, we must also reckon that the heat and immediacy of our disputes does not help the gentle and temperate spirit of our polity. It is too easy—through e-mail and other modes of electronic communication—to respond immediately to our neighbour. And not, as the marriage service has it, after serious, considered, and sober thought. This is a pity, because as many Anglicans know—or at least come to understand—much of our identity is better understood as implicit, not explicit. Moreover, we only reflect on our identity when under pressure, or in difficulty. And by then, it is often too late to rediscover the *via media*, because lines have already been drawn. This is unfortunate, because godly compromise and inclusiveness is part of our polity's soul. Our problems begin, as a church, when we try to be too overly defined; our genius, as a church, lies in our incompleteness and contestability. We are a humble church—still being formed. This is why resolutions and articles still feel alien to our soul. We are a church that is on the *viaticum*—still becoming.

It is perhaps no accident that when Jesus turned his metaphorically disposed mind to the subject of the church, he reached for a rather riveting analogy: "I am the vine, you are the branches." It is a suggestive, economic phrase, where one suspects that the use of the plural [branches] is quite deliberate. Even for an apparently homogenous organisation like the Church of England (let alone the Anglican Communion), "branches" offers a better descriptive fit than most of the labels on offer. It suggests intradependence yet difference; unity and diversity; commonality yet independence; continuity and change; pruning, yet fruitfulness.

In other words, the analogy sets up a correlation between particularity and catholicity. This is, of course, a struggle that Anglicans are all too familiar with. There is a constant wrestling for the "true" identity of Anglicanism; a struggle to reach a point where its soul ceases to be restless, and becomes more fully self-conscious. But in the meantime, the church finds itself easy prey to a variety of interest-led groups (from the theological left and right) that continually assert their freedoms over any uneasy consensus. The assumption made here is that any one branch is "free" from the others. Technically, this is correct. But the illusion of independence threatens to impoverish a profound catholic aspect of Anglicanism. The right to express and practice particularity is too often preferred to the self-imposed restraint that is hinted at by a deeper catholicity.

Thus, one branch will exercise its assumed privilege of freedom—whether that is fiscal, political, theological, or moral—over the others. The consequence of this is all too obvious. The branches attempt to define the vine. But this won't do. Which is why issues of gender, sexuality, and polity quickly become the primary foci that distinguish one branch from another, rather than secondary indicators of emphasis that are subjugated to an innate connectedness to the true vine. There seems to be little understanding that an unfettered claim to act freely can actually become antisocial, or even unethical. With great freedom comes even greater responsibility.

Interestingly, this is why bishops may have a vital role here in presiding over diversity whilst maintaining unity. Indeed, this is why the key to some of the current divisive Anglican dilemmas may lie in dioceses and provinces becoming more consciously expressive of their catholic identity, and celebrating their coherence amidst their diversity. A diocese is more than an arbitrary piece of territory. It is a part of a larger, living, organic whole. It is a branch of the vine. Therefore, exercising its freedom and expressing its particularity is less important than maintaining its connectedness. The trouble starts when any specific branch purports to speak and act for the whole, but without sufficient humility. Naturally, such restraint need not impose limits on diversity. It merely asks that the consequences of exercising one's freedom be more fully weighed.

The key to the future, dare one say it, may lie in balance. As we look forward to the next Lambeth Conference in 2018, there will be much to contemplate. How to hold together in the midst of tense, even bitter diversity? How to be one, yet many? How to be faithfully catholic, yet authentically local? Indeed, in finding the point of balance, we might discover that not all balancing points lie in the centre. In some balancing, the weights are always unequal, and the balancing point will be far to the left or the right of any equation. But finding that point is crucial, and it is normally motivated out of a deep sense of catholicity, rather than perhaps any slightly weaker sense of equitable fairness.

Ultimately, wisdom is more than mere reasonableness. Wisdom is not necessarily having our own sense of rights and justice vindicated, or our interests merely balanced. In our churches and Communion, ecclesial intelligence—wisdom—is about finding some points of balance in which much may be ceded by one party, or much may be gained by another. Compromise is sometime total, and not a halfway house. To compromise is to co-promise—do something together for a greater good, in which I or others may give more than is returned—at least in the immediate present and future. For Anglicans, giving and receiving to find balance will depend on the weight of the matters in hand, and on the weight of glory we can discern together. The weight and measure of Anglicanism is variable over time, cultures, and issues; and so are our points of balance. In all of this, and in striving for the true balance of *koinonia*, Anglicans may well discover that an ethic of *shared restraint*—borne out of a deep catholicity—may have much to offer the Anglican Communion in the present and future. Without this, Anglicans risk being painfully lost in the issues that beset the church—unable to see the wood for the trees. Or perhaps, as Jesus might have said, unable to see the vine for the branches?

# INDEX